Prehistoric Settlement in the South Pacific Coast of Chiapas, Mexico

PAPERS

of the

NEW WORLD ARCHAEOLOGICAL FOUNDATION

NUMBER SEVENTY-ONE

Prehistoric Settlement in the South Pacific

Coast of Chiapas, Mexico

by

Barbara Voorhies, Janine Gasco, and Paul Cackler

NEW WORLD ARCHAEOLOGICAL FOUNDATION

BRIGHAM YOUNG UNIVERSITY

PROVO, UTAH

2011

VOLUME EDITOR

MARY E. PYE

Printed by
BYU PRESS
PROVO, UTAH
2011

PREFACE

This is a report about archaeological investigations that we conducted in the late 1970s and early 1980s within a circumscribed area of the coastal plain in Chiapas, Mexico. We named the project "Proyecto Soconusco," after the general region in which the study took place. The senior author directed the project. It involved three field seasons, all substantially supported by successive grants from the National Geographic Society (#1932-78, #2257-80, #2534-82). Voorhies secured additional funds from the National Science Foundation (#78-07664) and from the Academic Senate of the University of California. The fieldwork was carried out under the auspices of the Consejo de Arqueología, Instituto Nacional de Antropología e Historia. We are grateful to the members of the Consejo and particularly to its three successive presidents who presided during the time of this project: José Luis Lorenzo, Angel García Cook and Joaquín García-Bárcena.

The New World Archaeological Foundation, Brigham Young University, provided crucial logistical support. In particular, this institution provided equipment, storage facilities for archaeological materials, and laboratory space for the analysis phase of this project. We are especially indebted to the late Gareth W. Lowe and Thomas A. Lee for this support and more generally for their collegiality and sage advice.

The archaeological field assistants responsible for much of the work reported here are Ann C. Bennett, John P. Carpenter, Andrea Gerstle, Lynette Heller, Dorothy Hosler, James M. Kules, Jack Mallory, Hector Neff, Linda Pfeiffer, Esther Schulsinger, and Clare Yarborough. Janine Gasco, one of the volume's co-authors, was also a field assistant and research assistant during all phases of this study. Several of these former graduate student assistants have now become well-known archaeologists. Other much appreciated assistance at various phases during the project was provided by Karen Buehler, Geoff Fuller, Howard Gard, Gary Graham, Walter H. Gerstle, Felipe Jacome, Miriam Jaffe, Kevin Kiper, Manasendu Kundu, Melissa Kurtz, Stephen Levy, Susan Medaris, Candace Neil, Richard Perry, Steven Ross, and M. Louise Sandy. Mary Hartman analyzed the human skeletal remains from Las Morenas and Linda Pfeiffer did the analysis of the human remains from Río Arriba.

Most of the maps in this volume were hand drafted by Alison Nethery who produced them in the early 1980s. Several additional illustrations were drafted much more recently by Aura de Anda working with computer software.

Voorhies's Research Assistants Kristi Butterwick and Paul Cackler at the University of Colorado, Boulder, and Sara Grasso and Amy Gusick at the University of California, Santa Barbara performed valued editorial services when we were finalizing the manuscript. In addition, Paul Cackler researched and wrote Chapter 6, which earned him co-authorship.

Finally, we are profoundly indebted to John E. Clark for catching several egregious errors in the text, as well as to Mary E. Pye and Arlene Colman for their editorial expertise, unswerving good humor, and steadfast patience throughout the process of assembling this monograph.

CONTENTS

FIGURES

TABLES

CHAPTER 1

METHODS OF SITE RECONNAISSANCE AND DATING

This is a report of archaeological investigations conducted within a delimited area on the south Pacific coast of southern Mexico, in the state of Chiapas. The study, dubbed "Proyecto Soconusco," was designed to retrieve basic settlement information for all identifiable ancient occupations within the study area. At the time this project began there was scant information about the overall settlement history of the Chiapas coastal plain, and no systematic settlement survey had been undertaken in the specific area of our investigations. Nonetheless, both Drucker (1948) and Navarrete (n.d.) had previously carried out casual archaeological surveys of the area, and their findings were very useful for our own work.

Proyecto Soconusco entailed three field seasons (Voorhies and Gasco 2004:9). During the first season, in 1978-79, we conducted a survey designed to locate archaeological sites. At this time we not only found archaeological sites on the landscape but whenever possible we mapped their surface features. During the second season, in 1981, we continued to map sites discovered in the previous season, and we tested a few sites. The third season, in 1983, focused entirely on the archaeological site of Acapetahua where we conducted a fairly extensive program of excavation (see Voorhies and Gasco 2004).

The area chosen for this study is situated on the coastal plain of the state of Chiapas. This is a broad, flat, low-lying alluvial plain that is bounded on the landward side by the escarpment of the Sierra Madre de Chiapas. Some minor foothills lie between the coastal plain and the mountains but along this stretch of the Pacific coast the foothills are not well developed. Seasonal and perennial wetlands occur along the seaward edge of the coastal plain. The coastal plain between the wetlands and the foothills is quite uniform topographically, except for the

rivers that transect the plain at fairly regular intervals. These rivers are not deeply incised but carry huge quantities of water during some rainy seasons (Voorhies and Kennett 1995).

The Proyecto Soconusco study area is an arbitrarily defined 755 sq km rectangular area lying between the principal coastal highway (Route 200) and the ocean (Figure 1.1) and centered on the municipality of Acapetahua. Our study area also incorporates small portions of the adjacent municipalities of Escuintla, Acacoyagua, Villa Comaltitlán, and Mapastepec. The study area encompasses some foothills along the inland border as well as a strip of coastal wetlands along the seaward margin, but the coastal plain constitutes the greatest portion of the area. Ultimately, we recorded 96 archaeological sites within the study area. These sites are the subjects of the present report.

We have two principal objectives in this report. First, we aim to describe the location, size and site layout of each site, note the duration of its occupation, and provide a map of surface features whenever appropriate. For most sites in our inventory this basic descriptive information has never been published, but in some cases such information has appeared in print. For example, detailed discussion of Late Archaic period sites in the study area has been published by Voorhies (2004) and a similar discussion for the Late Postclassic period sites is available in Voorhies and Gasco (2004). In instances where information about a particular site has already appeared in print we keep our descriptions brief and provide the appropriate reference.

The second objective in this present work is to tease out any salient patterns in settlement for different times during the known prehistory of the area under study. In an earlier publication Voorhies (1989b) discussed the number of sites and their spatial distributions over time in the

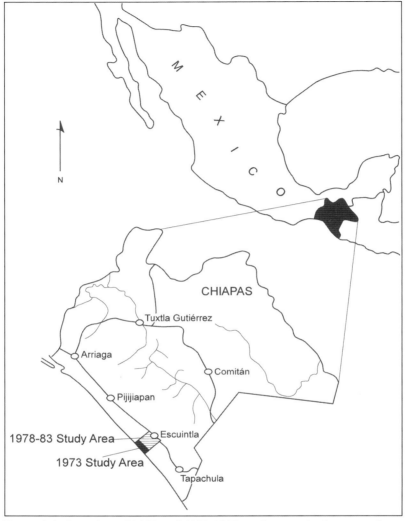

Figure 1.1. Location of 1973 and 1978-1983 study areas in the state of Chiapas, Mexico.

study area. Here, we try to identify regularities in intrasite architectural layouts for selected time periods and to address the issue of sociopolitical organization as deduced from settlement data. These latter topics are addressed in the final chapter of this publication.

Now, however, we present a discussion of our survey and dating methods. This information appeared previously in Voorhies (1989b). We have chosen to repeat some of this information in the present volume for the sake of completeness and the convenience of the reader.

SITE RECONNAISSANCE

As discussed in Voorhies (1989b) the methods that we adopted to locate archaeological sites included both formal, systematic procedures and informal procedures. The informal procedures were carried out concurrently with other activities throughout the entire first nine-month field season. They consisted of asking local people about the locations of archaeological sites and keeping a sharp eye out for sites as the field crew traveled by truck along the back roads of the area. These techniques were clearly the most efficient means of site recovery, but because they are unsystematic they have the disadvantage of precluding the calculation of site densities, one of the project objectives (Voorhies 1989b). Consequently, we also used systematic procedures of site discovery and these differed for each of the two major environmental zones of the area, i.e., the wetlands and terra firma (which includes both the coastal plain and the foothills).

Wetlands

The wetlands consist of a mangrove forest formation and patches of freshwater marsh associated with an extensive estuary and lagoon system (Voorhies 1976, 2004). The mangrove forest is well developed with trees reaching a height of 35 m. Cattails dominate the marsh ecozones and are most extensive farthest from the lagoon-estuary system's outlet. Habitable land within the wetlands is formed by inactive barrier beaches and by islands formed by human agents. These wetlands comprise 241 sq km, which is somewhat less than one third of the total area (755 sq km) investigated by us.

The method that we used for the systematic survey of the wetlands was to identify the locations of islands using aerial photographs and then to ground check these geomorphologic features for possible archaeological sites. This method is based on the assumption that prehistoric occupation of the wetlands was restricted to island locations. This untested assumption is based on the distribution of present day settlements that are found only on islands and was influenced by the impracticability of underwater research in this estuarine environment.

Prior to our fieldwork, we systematically examined stereoscopic pairs of aerial photographs (taken in 1964 by the S.R. H. Comisión del Grijalva by Aerofotogrametria, S.A.) with a Bausch and Lomb 240 Stereoscope and also with the unaided eye. By these means we identified locations that on the basis of photo imagery appeared to be islands. In a few instances the use of the stereoscope enabled us to detect photographic images of actual archaeological sites already known to us, but usually the scale of the photos (ca. 1:28,000), the relatively low elevations of site features, and the dense vegetation combined to prevent the detection of actual sites by means of visual examination of the photographs alone.

Once in the field, the archaeological team ground checked most locations where photo imagery indicated the presence of dry land within the wetlands. The results of this procedure are shown on the accompanying map (Figure 1.2). Island locations are indicated by shading, archaeological sites are plotted with specific symbols depending on the site type (discussed below).

We found archaeological sites on almost all islands that were significantly higher than water level at the time of survey. The major exception to this generalization is the back slope of the active beach, which, although as much as several meters higher than the water level, was devoid of archaeological remains. This sandy beach habitat was also uninhabited at the time of the survey except for one or two isolated houses but now, in 2008, it supports a row of rustic restaurants. Other uninhabited locations are the low-lying islands situated in the southwestern portion of the study area between small channels of the waterway. These islands are not occupied at the present time and also lacked prehistoric remains.

Most of the wetland archaeological sites fall into either one of two major categories: isolated mounds formed by the gradual accumulation of debris (shell mounds and earthen mounds), and sites with multiple artificial platform mounds. As we discuss below these two categories of sites differ in their occupational histories and functional significance. Several wetland sites fit neither of the two site categories and these are discussed in Appendix B under the heading of Miscellaneous Sites.

All of the accumulative mounds in the wetlands are currently islands. Five of these, all shell mounds, have been reported by Voorhies (1976; 2004) and date to the Late Archaic period. The remaining sites are earthen mounds that apparently were initially formed during

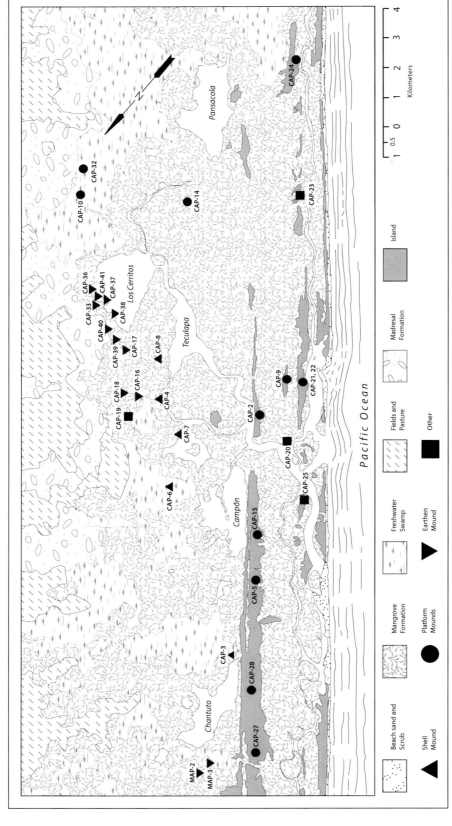

Figure 1.2. Wetland zone of the Proyecto Soconusco study area showing the locations of biotic zones, islands, and archaeological sites.

the Preclassic period. Most earthen mounds are located near the interface between the mangrove formation and the *madresal* formation, that is, near the boundary between continuously and periodically inundated forests. Single earthen mounds are also clustered on the inland side of the lagoons Teculapa and Los Cerritos (Figure 1.2).

The second major class of sites found in the wetlands consists of multiple artificial platform mounds positioned on naturally formed islands. Each of the relatively large, elevated islands formed by inactive barrier beaches tends to support at least one of these sites (Figure 1.2). These multiple mound sites are morphologically similar to sites located on the dry land portion of the study area and because of this it is instructive to compare the site densities of the two zones.

In order to calculate density figures for the platform mound sites in the wetlands, it is necessary to determine the area of inhabitable land within the wetland environment. This objective was met by an assistant, Geoff Fuller, who measured the areas of twenty-seven islands on the base map of the wetland area and calculated their actual sizes. The islands that were measured are those shown with shading on Figure 1.2. Fuller used a digital planimeter and averaged three measurements for each of the islands. The results are listed in Table 1.1. The total area for the islands is approximately 11 sq km. Since eleven sites with artificial platforms have been recorded within the wetlands, this gives a site density in the wetland environment of one site per sq km, when islands only are considered (Voorhies 1989b).

Terra firma

The portion of the study area accessible during the dry season by land transportation is considered here as terra firma. It consists of three geomorphologic zones that form irregularly linear ecozones parallel to the coastline. These zones, from the inland edge of the wetlands toward the mountains, are the following: 1) a flat portion of the coastal plain that is seasonally flooded; 2) a flat portion of the coastal plain that is drained by rivers; and

Table 1.1. Areas in square kilometers of 27 islands in the wetlands (from Voorhies 1989b:Table 5.2).

Island No.	Area (km²)
1	0.172
2	0.060
3	0.093
4	0.056
5	4.734
6	0.081
7	0.055
8	0.040
9	0.051
10	0.045
11	0.177
12	0.045
13	0.034
14	0.126
15	0.186
16	2.346
17	0.288
18	0.148
19	0.190
20	0.841
21	0.376
22	0.095
23	0.023
24	0.028
25	0.039
26	0.062
27	0.528
Total Area (km²):	10.919

Table 1.2. Area measurements of each sampling universe in terra firma, area of sampled portions of each universe, and percent of the sampled portion of each universe (from Voorhies 1989b:Table 5.3).

Universe	Universe area (km²)	Sampled area (km²)	Percent of universe area sampled
A	50.19	1.74	3.47
B	51.50	4.46	8.66
C	29.75	2.33*	7.83
D	45.81	1.61	3.51
E	48.50	3.91	8.06
F	82.62	7.61	9.21
G	86.94	3.88	4.62
H	72.44	5.91	8.16
I	46.88	2.21^	4.71
Totals	514.63	33.66	6.47

*Excluding the portion of C-4 that falls in Universe I.

^Including the portion of C-4 that falls in Universe I.

3) hills that comprise the piedmont of the Sierra Madre de Chiapas. The total area of *terra firma* within the study area is 515 sq km (Table 1.2).

All exploration within the terra firma portion of the study area involved visual inspection at ground level. In addition to the informal methods of crew observation and the use of informants, systematic ground reconnaissance was achieved by walking transects. This method resulted in on-the-ground coverage of 33.66 sq km, that is, the pedestrian survey covered 6.47 percent of terra firma in the study area (Table 1.2; Voorhies 1989b).

The method of sampling involved stratifying the area into sampling universes, plotting each universe with transect lines, and selecting some of these lines from each universe for on-the-ground inspection. These operations will be described in detail.

The terra firma portion of the study area was stratified into nine sampling universes indicated by the letters A through I (Figure 1.3). The determining factor in the delimitation of these universes was the necessity that each universe be bounded on two opposite sides by roads. This was required by the logistics of crew drop-off and pick-up at transect termini and resulted in the formation of sampling universes of different shapes and sizes. An ideal arrangement would have been to have equal shapes and sizes for all universes but such an arrangement would have been extremely impractical because of the poor accessibility of most parts of the study area. The arrangement of the sampling universes is shown on Figure 1.3, and their sizes are given in Table 1.2. Sizes range from approximately 30 sq km (Universe C) to approximately 87 sq km (Universe G).

After the area had been stratified using a base map at the scale of 1:100,000, Voorhies plotted transect lines at regular intervals across each universe. These lines were oriented in the cardinal directions whenever possible in order to simplify the logistics during the actual ground survey. The lines were plotted at intervals of 1 km. The goal for each transect was for the field crew to cover a swath that was 500 m wide. This width was based on the ideal situation of having ten crewmembers spaced at 50 m intervals. This sampling strategy results in series of 500 m wide

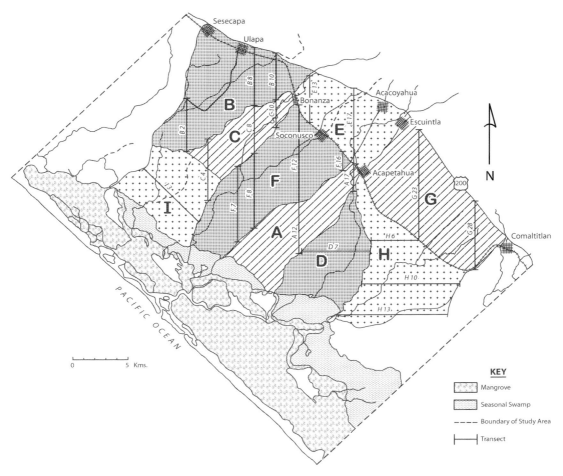

Figure 1.3. Proyecto Soconusco study area showing the mangrove forest, seasonal swamp, and, within terra firma, the locations of sampling universes. The transect lines that were surveyed are labeled with a letter and number designation (from Voorhies 1989b:Fig. 5.3).

strips that are potential transects but which are separated from each other by 500 m that have been excluded from the sample.

Using a random numbers table Voorhies chose transects to be field surveyed. In a few instances Voorhies rejected the first random number selected because the transect lay along a road where visual inspection could be carried out more efficiently by crewmembers traveling by truck. In such cases a second choice was made through the use of a random numbers table.

The ideal plan for surveying selected transects was never fully achieved during the on-the-ground reconnaissance. Problems included crew member absenteeism resulting in a smaller than ten member crew, the necessity for crew members to close rank because of dense impenetrable brush, and the occasional straying of one or more crew members from the rest of the team. These problems occurred without warning and usually could not be corrected in the field. As a result the day's activities did not conform entirely to plan. The individual maps of the transects have been drawn to reflect any such problems that were encountered. That is, in as much as possible, they reflect actual rather than ideal circumstances.

The field crews always had two leaders in the pedestrian surveys. One leader's responsibility was to keep the team on the correct compass bearing. The other leader was in charge of plotting the actual progress of the crew on aerial photographs so that an accurate record of the terrain covered was maintained. These plotted transects (Figs. 1.6 to 2.6) form the database for determining actual areas covered by survey crews. These determinations were made in Santa Barbara using a digital planimeter.

Table 1.3 displays the results of systematic ground reconnaissance within terra firma. Twenty-two sites were found within the approximately 34 sq km covered by the survey crew. This gives a study area average of 0.65 sites per square kilometer for the terra firma sector (Voorhies 1989b). Note that this site density is less than that calculated for the multiple mound sites in the wetland portion of the study area.

It can be seen also on Table 1.3 that site density varies within the terra firma sector of the study area. Although apparently fairly uniform over the well-drained portion of the coast (that is, the foothills and the coastal plain), the seasonally inundated zone was clearly avoided. Only a few sites (e.g., COM-2) are within this zone but these are very scarce as can be seen on Fig. 1.4. Present day inhabitants of the study area generally avoid this zone for their residences. Those people who do live in the zone are frequently forced to evacuate their homes during the rainy season.

DATING THE SITES

As mentioned, at the end of the site reconnaissance phase of Proyecto Soconusco we had 96 sites in our inventory. The locations of these sites are plotted on Figure 1.4. We mapped all sites with surface features, and whenever possible we collected artifacts from the site surfaces. In most cases the surface collections were simply grab samples of lithic and ceramic artifacts, that is, we used no systematic sampling strategy when making these collections. The reason for this is that in most cases we found very few artifacts on the site surface. In a few cases, where abundant surface material was found (e.g., CAP-32 and CAP-1), we were able to maintain separate collections for individual mounds.

We used potsherds to identify the times that individual sites were occupied. To do this we relied on ceramic chronologies that had been developed by investigators working in nearby areas, particularly those in the publications and comparative collections of the New World Archaeological Foundation curated in the facilities in San Cristóbal de las Casas, Chiapas. As our understanding of the local chronology improved due to the results of the subsurface excavations at some sites, we continually refined the local ceramic sequence. Still, we were able to employ only broad temporal categories, i.e., periods, because more precise temporal units such as phases had not been defined when we carried out our study.

Of course we were not able to use ceramics to establish the age of Archaic period sites since this time period predates the adoption of pottery in Mesoamerica. The other time period for which almost no ceramics have been identified is the Early Postclassic period. We simply have been unable to get a "fix" on the ceramic assemblage for this time period on the basis of the surface and subsurface materials, and this results in a major analytical problem (See Voorhies and Gasco [2004] for a discussion of this problem). The best known Early Postclassic period diagnostic, Tohil Plumbate, is difficult to distinguish from earlier plumbate unless whole vessels are available for study or paste analyses are performed on sherds (Neff 1984). At least one of these conditions was met at only four sites. For example, a whole Tohil Plumbate pot was recovered by the owner of the Campíto site (CAP-15), and this vessel is now housed in the Museo de Antropología, Tuxtla Gutiérrez, Chiapas. Similarly, Drucker (1948:159) illustrates an apparent Tohil vessel from La Concepción (CAP-24). Moreover, neutron activation analysis on sherds from both Las Morenas (MAP-5) and Río Arriba (CAP-32) indicates the presence of Tohil Plumbate (Neff, personal communication). It may be significant that these sites are all

Table 1.3. Summary of survey data from pedestrian transects (from Voorhies 1989b:Table 5.4).

Transect	Sites	No. of sites	Area (km²)	Sites/(km²)
A-12	CAP-45; CAP-30; CAP-31	3	1.00	3.00
A-17		0	0.74	0.00
Total Area (km²)			1.74	
B-2	CAP-72; MAP-4	2	1.37	1.46
B-8	CAP-50; CAP-49; CAP-54	3	2.03	1.48
B-10		0	1.06	0.00
Total Area (km²)			4.46	
C-4	CAP-51; CAP-29	2	0.88*	2.27
C-8		0	0.70	0.00
C-10		0	0.75	0.00
Total Area (km²)			2.33	
D-7	CAP-58	1	1.61	0.62
E-13		0	1.32	0.00
E-17	CAC-9; CAC-7; CAC-8; CAP-63	4	2.59	1.54
Total Area (km²)			7.61	
F-7		0	1.54	0.00
F-8		0	2.54	0.00
F-12	CAP-69; CAP-70; CAP-68	3	3.07	0.98
F-16		0	0.46	0.00
Total Area (km²)			7.61	
G-23	ESC-5	1	2.62	0.38
G-28	ESC-7; ESC-6; COM-4	3	1.26	0.38
Total Area (km²)			3.88	
H-6		0	0.60	0
H-10		0	1.86	0
H-13		0	3.45	0
Total Area (km²)			5.91	
I-3		0	1.73	0
I-X		0	0.48	0
Total Area (km²)			2.21	
COLUMN TOTALS		22	33.66	0.65

*Excluding portion of C-4 that falls within survey area I.

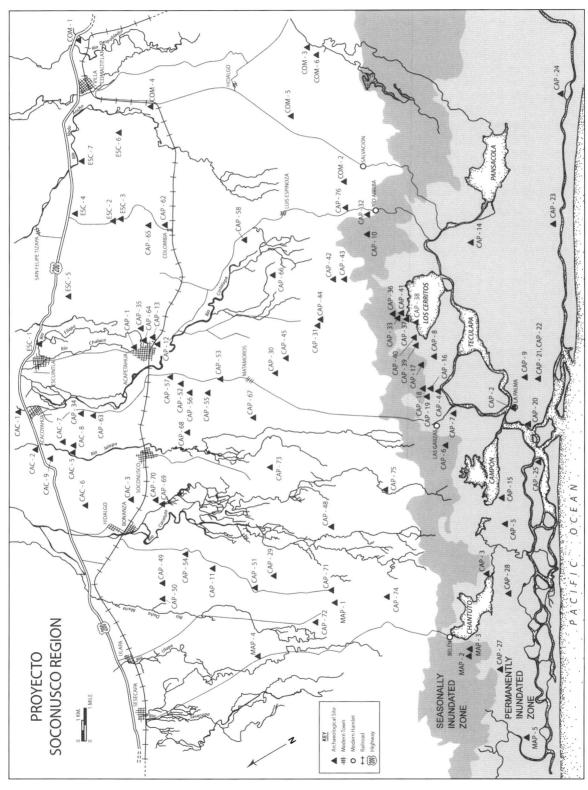

Figure 1.4. Map of the Proyecto Soconusco study area showing all documented archaeological sites (drafted by A. Nethery; from Voorhies 1989b:Fig. 5.6).

positioned in the lower gradient of the coastal plain, within or adjacent to the wetlands. It is important to emphasize, however, that we did not systematically test all plumbate sherds collected from site surfaces for the possibility of Tohil Plumbate.

The Early Postclassic period for the south coast of Mesoamerica has been problematic (Voorhies and Gasco 2004:11ff) for some time and we regret that the present work contributes nothing to the resolution of some of these problems. Specifically, we would like to know whether there was an abrupt demographic crash during this time period or whether it is our inability to recognize sites from this period that results in the apparent small number of sites that were occupied during this time.

Ultimately, we were able to date 91 sites, or 95 percent of the total number of known sites in this survey. The site chronologies are displayed graphically in Figure 1.5. The relative intensity of each site occupation is indicated in this graph by the width of the bar. Intensity was estimated on the basis of the relative number of surface ceramics per time period, as well as a consideration of intrasite settlement patterns. We admit freely that this measure is highly subjective, but we think that it does convey an approximate idea about the relative importance of each site over the duration of its history.

One limitation regarding site dating is that the number of surface artifacts varied greatly, and in the majority of cases they were scarce. At the time of our study most sites had undisturbed surfaces, as plowing was not practiced widely in the area at that time. This meant that subsurface artifacts were not being brought readily to the present day ground level. Furthermore, many sites had a thick mantle of vegetation that obscured any surface artifacts. For these reasons we harbored serious doubts about whether the surface collections accurately reflected the buried deposits at the sites.

In order to evaluate the accuracy of our site dating based on surface ceramics we compare the results of the ages of surface ceramics with those excavated at the same sites. This was possible only at the sites that were excavated during the second and third field seasons of

Proyecto Soconusco. Table 1.4 summarizes these results.

The results displayed in the table increase our confidence that the dating of the Proyecto Soconusco sites is fairly reliable, but they also indicate that the assignments to time periods are not precisely accurate, as we suspected. We have data on temporally sensitive surface artifacts and subsurface artifacts for nine sites. In four sites (MAP-5, CAP-1, CAP-13, CAP-2) the results of the dated surface and subsurface ceramics are identical. In two other cases the surface survey produced dated ceramics from periods that are not represented in the excavated material. In these cases, CAP-55, COM-6, Late Postclassic period material was collected from site surfaces but was not found in the excavations. The site plans of these two sites are typical of those from the Classic period so we suspect that the Late Postclassic period occupation was very light and materials from that period did not become buried.

In any event, we are most concerned with the possibility that the surface collected materials do not include markers from occupational periods known to exist on the basis of dated ceramics from the excavations. This occurred in three cases, but in one of these cases the implications are not very troublesome. At CAP-32, it was possible to identify Early Postclassic material only by means of sherd paste analysis, and that was done on some excavated sherds but not on the surface sherds. In light of the problems concerned with identifying artifacts from the Early Postclassic period this finding is not too unsettling. However, at CAP-35, a site with a distinctive Late Postclassic period settlement layout, an early Late Preclassic–Early Classic occupation identified in the excavations was not detected in the surface collection. This surface collection is small and only three ceramic types could be identified, so we have attributed this discrepancy to the small sample size. Accordingly, only at CAC-1 is there what we consider a serious discrepancy between the surface and subsurface dating, as Early and Middle Preclassic material was recovered from the excavations but was not identified in the surface collection. Nevertheless,

Figure 1.5. Chronological chart for Proyecto Soconusco sites. The width of each bar represents an estimate of the intensity of occupation for various time periods at each site. Sites absent from the chart could not be dated (after Voorhies 1989b:Fig. 5.7).

Table 1.4. Dates of diagnostic ceramics from site surfaces compared with dates of excavated ceramics from same sites.

Site	Dates of Surface Ceramics	Dates of Excavated Ceramics
Tepalcatenco (CAC-1)	Late Preclassic Protoclassic Early Classic Late Postclassic	Early, Middle, Late Preclassic Protoclassic Early Classic Late Postclassic
Las Morenas (MAP-5)	Late Preclassic Early, Middle, Late Classic Early, Late Postclassic	Late Preclassic Late Postclassic
Río Arriba (CAP-32; Pfeiffer 1983)	Early, Middle, Late Classic	Early, Middle, Late Classic Early Postclassic?
Acapetahua (CAP-1)	Late Preclassic Protoclassic Early, Middle, Late Classic Late Postclassic	Late Preclassic Protoclassic Early, Middle, Late Classic Late Postclassic
Rancho Alegre (CAP-55)	Middle, Late Classic Late Postclassic	Middle, Late Classic
Las Lomas (COM-6)	Classic Late Postclassic	Middle, Late Classic
Lomas Juana (CAP-35)	Late Postclassic	Late Preclassic Protoclassic Early Classic Late Postclassic
Filapa (CAP-13)	Late Preclassic Protoclassic Early, Middle, Late Classic Late Postclassic	Late Preclassic Protoclassic Early, Middle, Late Classic Late Postclassic
La Palma (CAP-2)	Classic Late Postclassic	Classic Late Postclassic

both lots suggest that the site is primarily Protoclassic in age with a light Late Postclassic period occupation. Our findings thus suggest that the surface dating may overlook minor buried components in 22 percent (two of nine) cases. In all cases the major occupations and most minor ones were correctly identified from the surface sherds.

As may be seen in Figure 1.5, the vast majority of dated sites were occupied over long stretches of time. In fact, only three sites (MAP-3, CAP-12, CAP-64) apparently have single components, and one of these sites is dated only tentatively. The rarity of single component sites prompts two further observations. First, it appears that the factors that made certain locations attractive for human occupation continued to be at play for long periods of time. Second, the prevalence of multicomponent sites complicates our endeavors to reconstruct regional settlement patterns for specific time periods. Despite this recognition, we attempt to do this in each of the chapters below.

ORGANIZATION OF THE PRESENT VOLUME

We have organized this presentation around individual time periods. We did this because our primary goal is to tease out intrasite and intersite settlement patterns for chronologically different occupations. Previously, Voorhies (1989b) published a series of regional maps for the study area that depicted the number and distribution of sites over the landscape for eight time intervals: the Archaic, Early-Middle Preclassic, Late Preclassic, Protoclassic, Early Classic, Middle Classic, Late Classic, and Late Postclassic periods. The published maps show sites in the study area for which occupancy of any given period has been identified by the study of chronologically diagnostic artifacts as we described above. These maps when viewed together show the rise and fall of the number of sites over time, as well as chronological changes in spatial distribution.

As mentioned above, almost all the sites in the inventory were occupied for two or more time periods, which presents us with a major challenge in trying to identify intrasite settlement layouts that are chronologically sensitive and can be attributed to any one particular time period. We reason that the site plans of platform-mound sites most likely document the appearance of the site during its last major occupation. So, for example, our premise is that the site plan of a hypothetical site occupied continuously from the Late Preclassic through the Late Classic periods most likely best reflects the site organization during the Late Classic period, the time of the site's last occupation. This is our justification for grouping the sites according to their last major occupation. In the cited example, we would describe the site in the chapter dedicated to sites with final occupations during the Late Classic period.

Chapter 2 presents information about sites that consist of mounds that have formed by the gradual buildup of sediments. These sites are the earliest ones in our survey, and they consist of shell mounds dating to the Late Archaic period and earthen mounds probably all dating to the Preclassic period. Chapter 3 presents information about sites that were last occupied during the Early Classic period. Not many sites fall into this category since most of the sites occupied during that time interval continued to be occupied throughout the rest of the Classic. Chapter 4 presents sites that had their final occupations in the Late Classic period and Chapter 5 reviews sites with their last significant occupations during the Late Postclassic period. In the final chapter we discuss intersite settlement patterns throughout the time covered by these data.

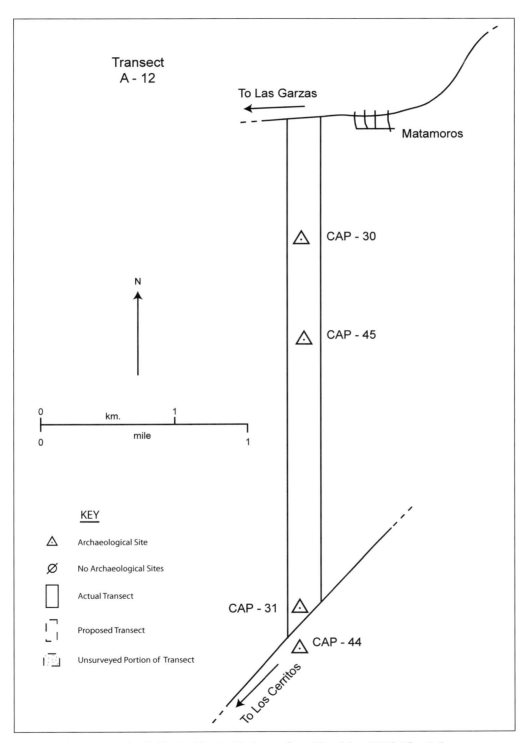

Figure 1.6. Transect A-12 (drafted by A. Nethery; from Voorhies 1989b:Fig. 5.4).

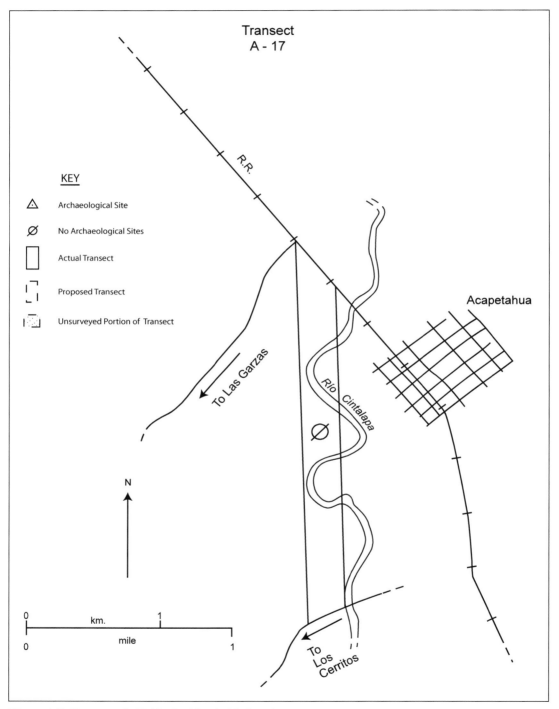

Figure 1.7. Transect A-17 (drafted by A. Nethery).

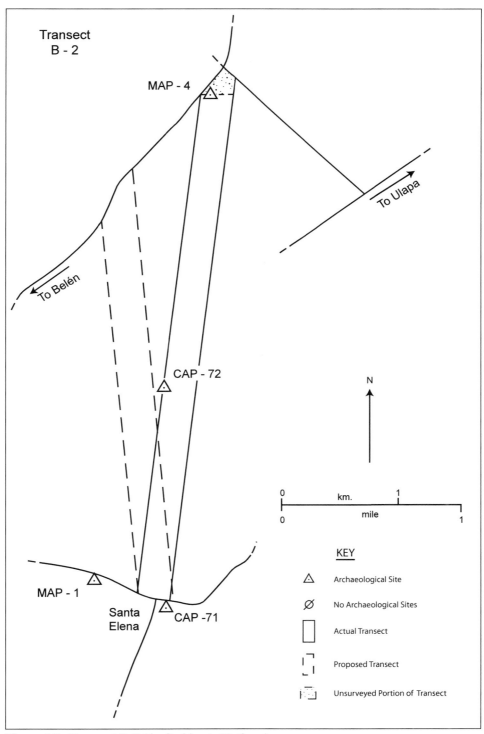

Figure 1.8. Transect B-2 (drafted by A. Nethery).

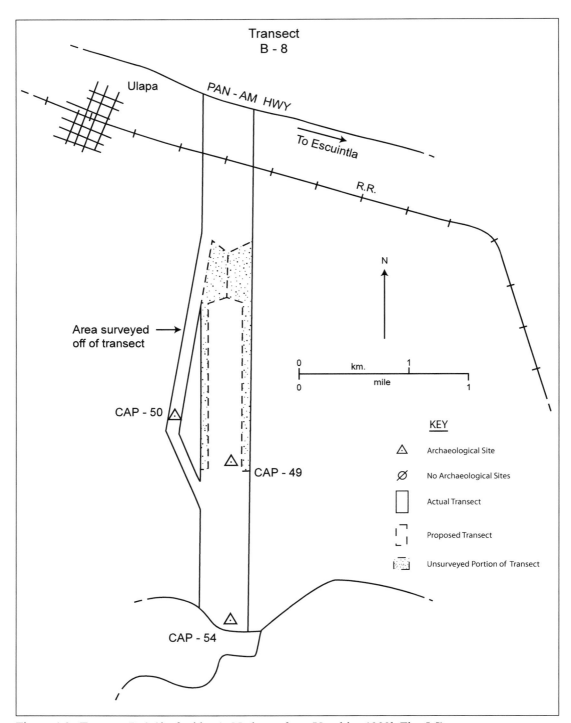

Figure 1.9. Transect B-8 (drafted by A. Nethery; from Voorhies 1989b:Fig. 5.5).

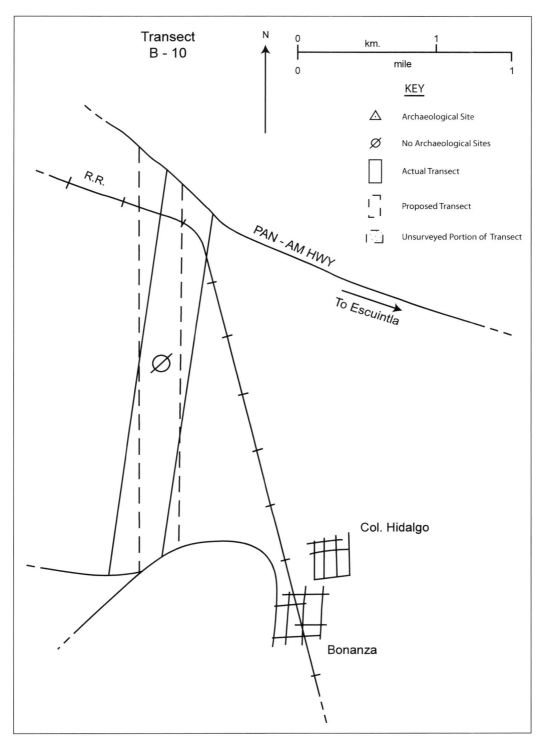

Figure 1.10. Transect B-10 (drafted by A. Nethery).

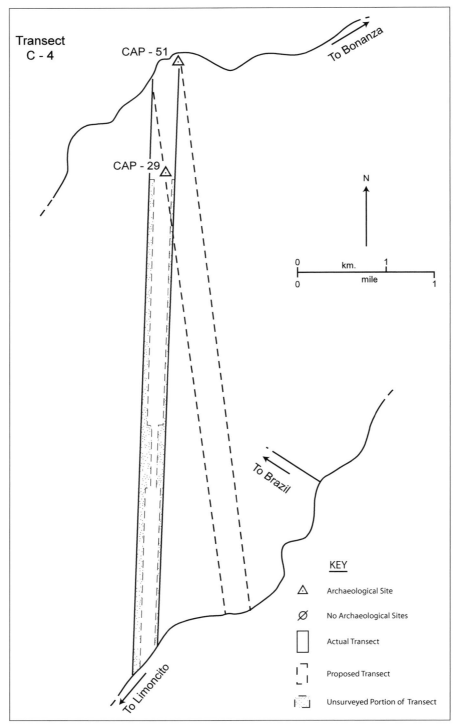

Figure 1.11. Transect C-4 (drafted by A. Nethery).

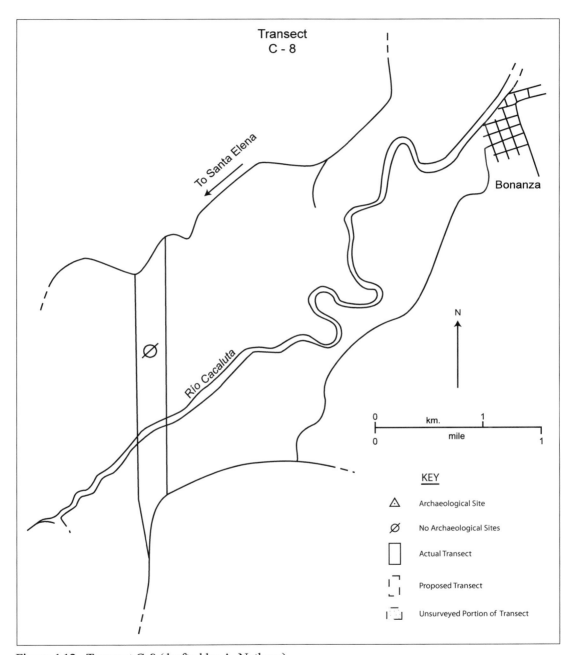

Figure 1.12. Transect C-8 (drafted by A. Nethery).

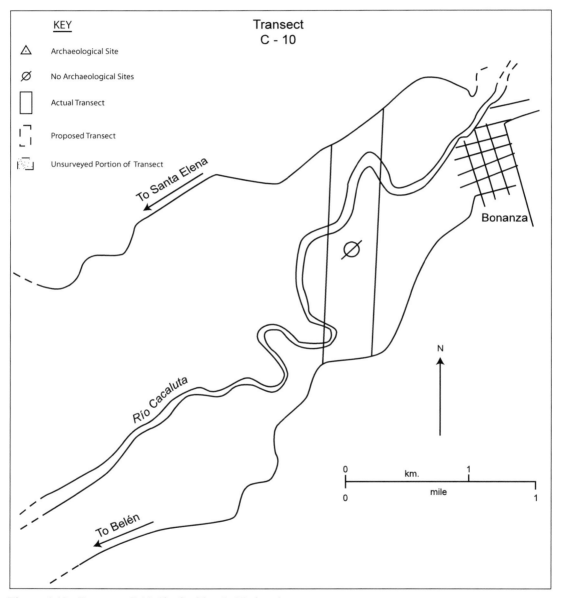

Figure 1.13. Transect C-10 (drafted by A. Nethery).

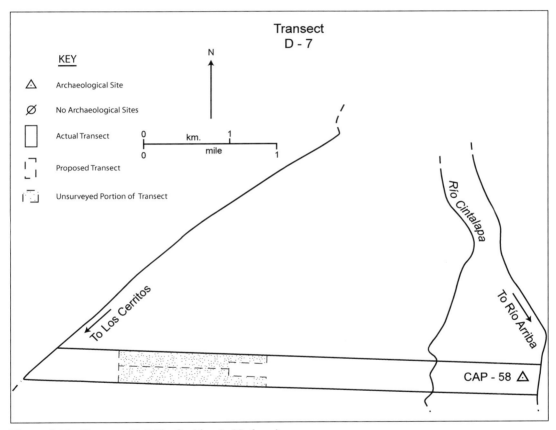

Figure 1.14. Transect D-7 (drafted by A. Nethery).

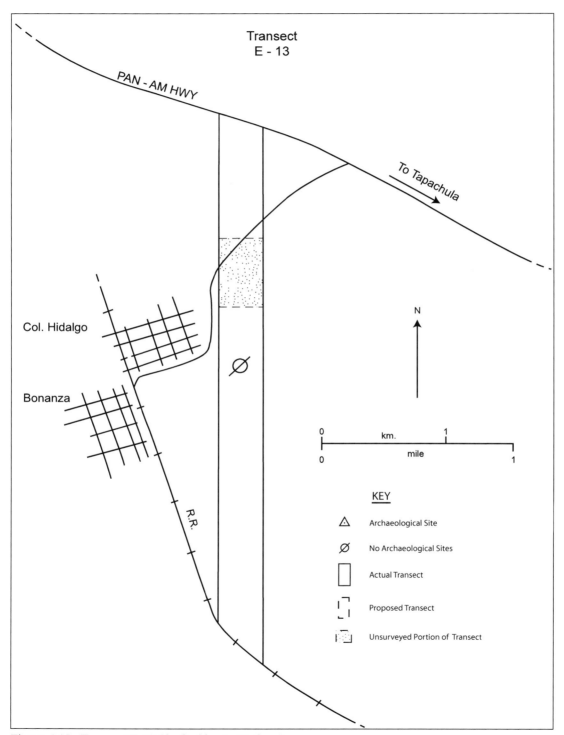

Figure 1.15. Transect E-13 (drafted by A. Nethery).

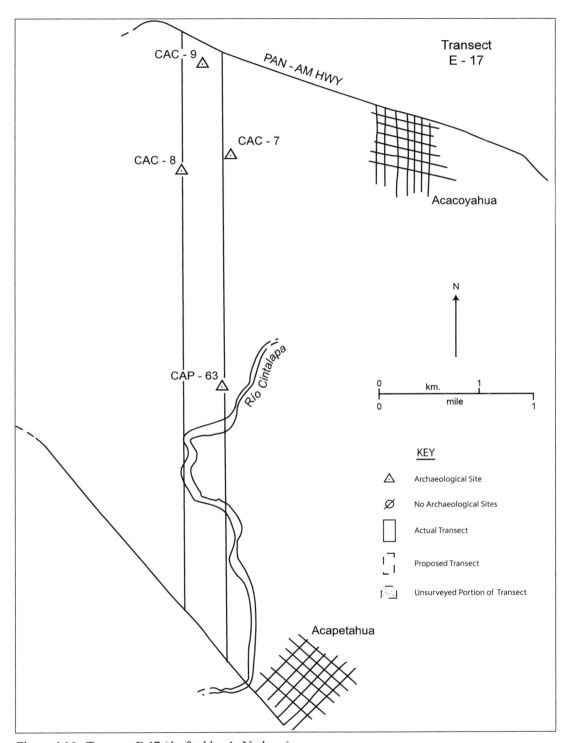

Figure 1.16. Transect E-17 (drafted by A. Nethery).

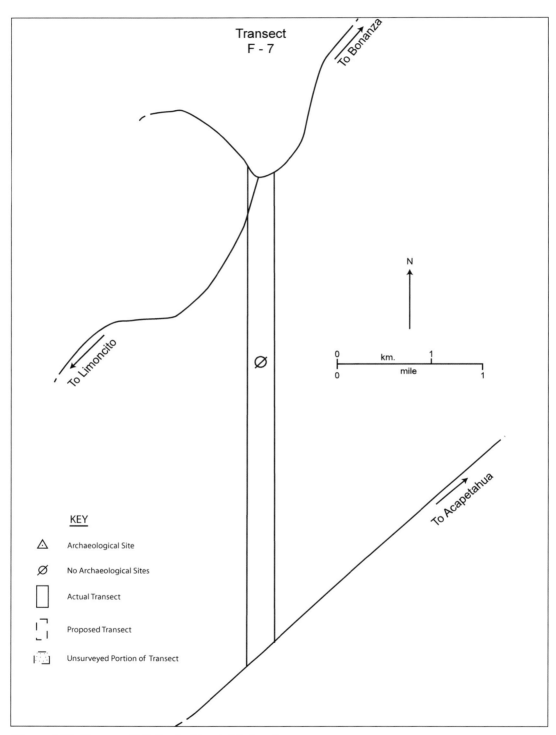

Figure 1.17. Transect F-7 (drafted by A. Nethery).

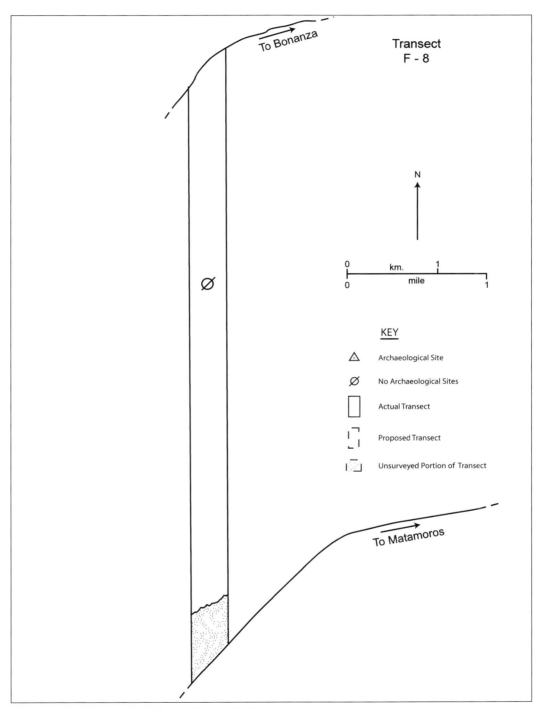

Figure 1.18. Transect F-8 (drafted by A. Nethery).

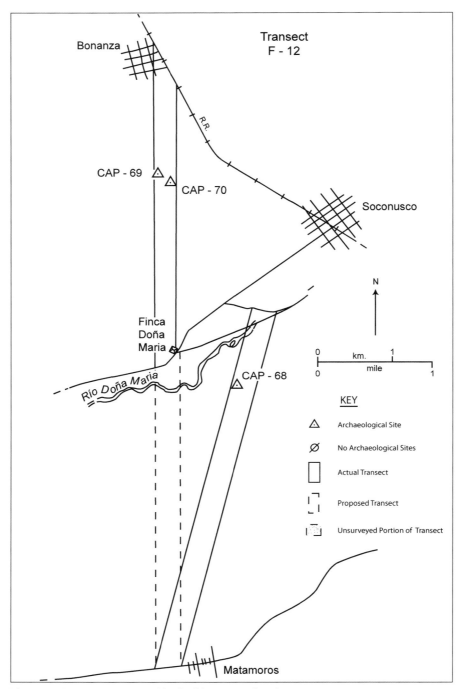

Figure 1.19. Transect F-12 (drafted by A. Nethery).

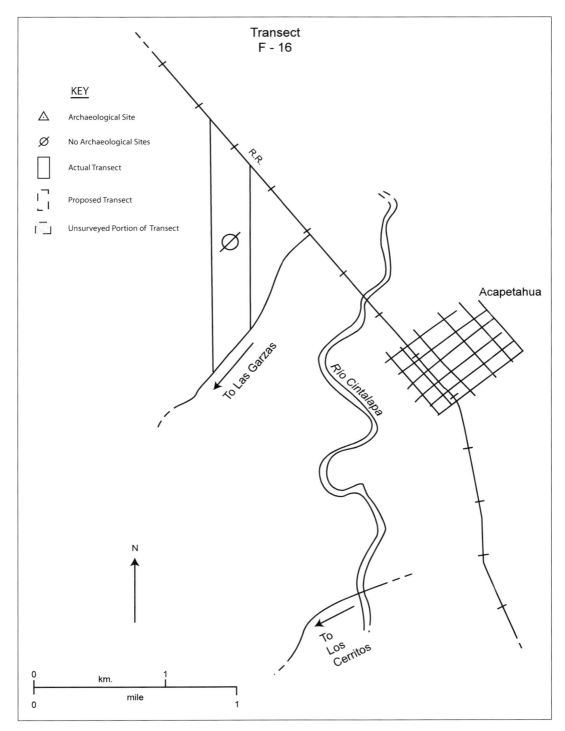

Figure 1.20. Transect F-16 (drafted by A. Nethery).

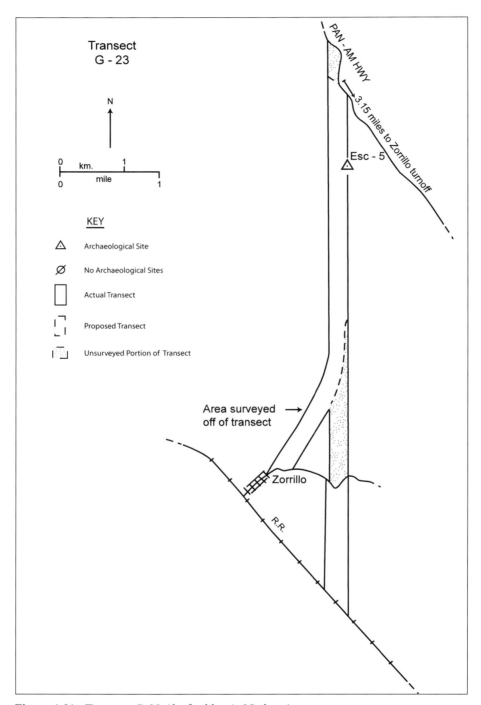

Figure 1.21. Transect G-23 (drafted by A. Nethery).

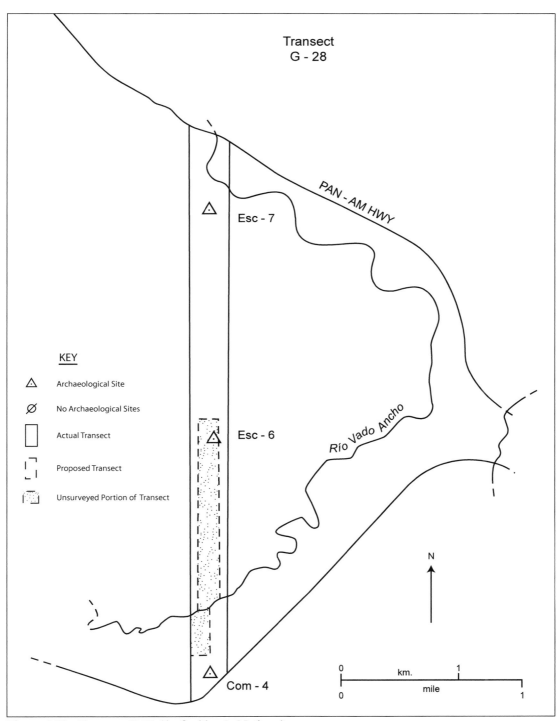

Figure 1.22. Transect G-28 (drafted by A. Nethery).

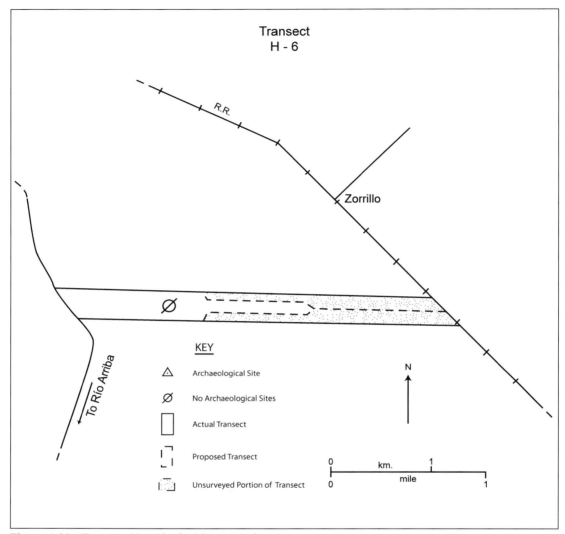

Figure 1.23. Transect H-6 (drafted by A. Nethery).

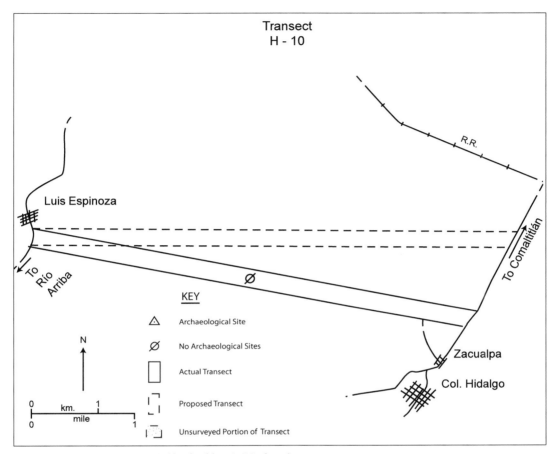

Figure 1.24. Transect H-10 (drafted by A. Nethery).

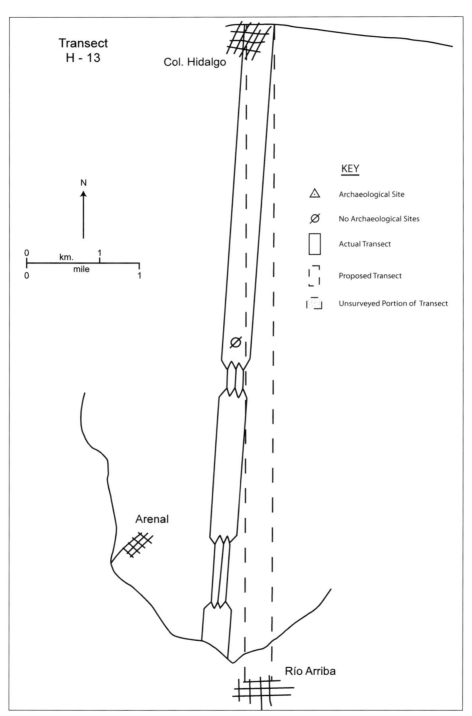

Figure 1.25. Transect H-13 (drafted by A. Nethery).

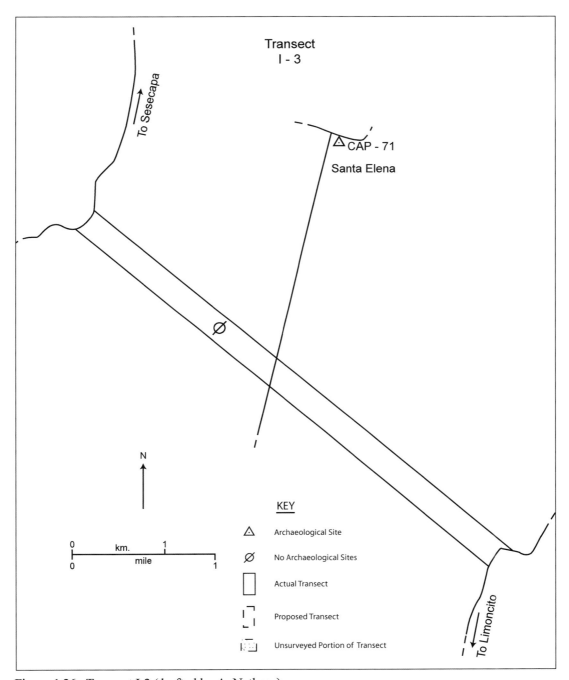

Figure 1.26. Transect I-3 (drafted by A. Nethery).

CHAPTER 2

ACCUMULATIVE MOUNDS

The Proyecto Soconusco field crew discovered 17 accumulative mounds, all of which are located in or near the wetlands, as we discussed in Chapter 1. Each of these mounds is an isolated feature that presumably formed by the gradual deposition of debris, rather than being an intentionally constructed platform. The inventory of accumulative mounds includes five shell mounds (Chantuto [CAP-3], Campón [CAP-6], Tlacuachero [CAP-7], El Chorro [CAP-4] and Zapotillo [CAP-8]), the core deposits of which are aceramic and known to date to the Late Archaic period (Figure 1.2). The remaining mounds in the inventory are earthen mounds. Archaeologists have investigated the subsurface contents of two of these, both of which (Los Cerritos [CAP-37] and El Grillo [CAP-16]) date to the Preclassic time period. At present it is difficult to determine whether the remaining earthen mounds also date to the Preclassic period, but we suspect that they do. Moreover, based on the surface collection of ceramics, it is known that many of these accumulative mounds were used for long periods of time regardless when they began to form.

The details of investigations at the shell mound sites are published elsewhere (e.g., Voorhies 1976, 2004; Voorhies et al. 2002). In addition to the five Late Archaic shell mounds in the present study area, there is an earlier mound farther to the south that is similar to them in most respects but dates to the Middle Archaic period (Voorhies et al. 2002; Voorhies 2004:81-100). In all cases, however, the core deposits of the shell mounds are formed of bedded marsh clam shells that occur in couplets, with each pair of strata consisting of a bed of unbroken shells and a bed of thermally altered shells. Voorhies interprets this internal structure, which is observed in the matrix of the six sites, as the signature of ancient clam bakes. In this view the shell mound sites functioned as processing locations for aquatic resources. Logistical foragers, named the Chantuto people by archaeologists, formed these sites. Radiocarbon age determinations place this entire occupation within the Middle to Late Archaic period (5500-1500 BC), but in the present study area only Late Archaic period shell mounds have been found. In all the studied shell mounds the Archaic period deposits are draped with a mantle of soil that contains potsherds. In general this upper stratum is highly bioturbated and the datable sherds are not in chronological order.

SHELL MOUNDS

The five shell mounds are briefly described below. The reader is encouraged to consult the cited sources for further information. We discuss the sites in the order that they are presented in the histogram (Figure 1.5), reading from left to right. We follow the same order of presentation in each of the subsequent chapters.

Campón (CAP-6)

This site is located within the mangrove forest east of Laguna Campón. Known locally as El Castaño, the site was first reported and named Campón by José Luis Lorenzo (1955). Lorenzo mapped the site but did not excavate it. Subsequently, Eduardo Martínez remapped the site, and Voorhies excavated three test pits (Voorhies 1976:39ff; 2004:80-81). The site area is 0.83 ha, and the highest elevation is slightly above 6 m (Figure 2.1). As determined by excavations, it was occupied from the Late Archaic period continuously through the Early Classic period. Surface materials included marsh clams and a few sherds.

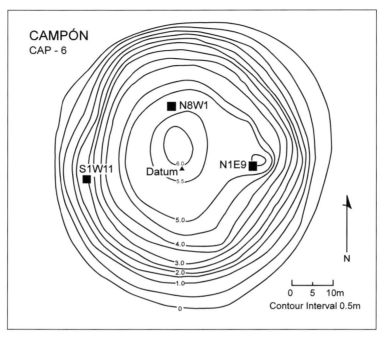

Figure 2.1. Topographic map of the Campón shell mound
(map by E. Martínez E.; from Voorhies 2004:Fig. 2.28).

Zapotillo (CAP-8)

This shell mound is located north of Laguna
Teculapa, within the mangrove formation. It
was initially discovered, mapped, and excavated
by Voorhies in 1971 (Voorhies 1976:34-36;
Voorhies 2004:76-80). The site is oval in outline
and symmetrical, with its highest elevation at
the center. It is 1.17 ha in area and is slightly
over 11 m high (Figure 2.2). Marsh clams and
potsherds are abundant on the surface.

In addition to the occupation during the
Archaic period, the site was in use continuously
from the Early Preclassic through the Late
Classic periods.

EL Chorro (CAP-4)

This site is located southeast of the
embarcadero Las Garzas alongside a canal
within the mangrove formation. Carlos
Navarrete discovered the site during his 1969
survey of the coast of Chiapas (personal
communication). The site is circular in outline
and symmetrical, with the highest point (> 5.5
m) near the site center (Figure 2.3). There are no
surface features. The mound's area is 0.20 ha.
Navarrete investigated the subsurface deposits
at the site in 1969, and Voorhies excavated it in
2005.

Navarrete (n.d.) dug three test pits that
he reported in a single generalized profile.
Potsherds were recovered from the upper levels
(to a maximum depth of 0.9 m). These were
dated as mainly from the Postclassic period,
with some Early Preclassic period artifacts.
Underlying the sherd-bearing layers were
aceramic strata sampled to depths of 2.0 and 2.5
m. This material is Late Archaic in age.

During the site reconnaissance reported
here, we identified occupations for the
Protoclassic-Late Classic time span based upon
the surface collection, in addition to the Archaic
period deposits.

Finally, in 2005, Voorhies excavated two
test pits in this shell mound, and Douglas
Kennett took a sediment core from the base
of the mound (Kennett et al. 2007). The
radiocarbon dates obtained from samples in the
core and excavations suggest that the mound

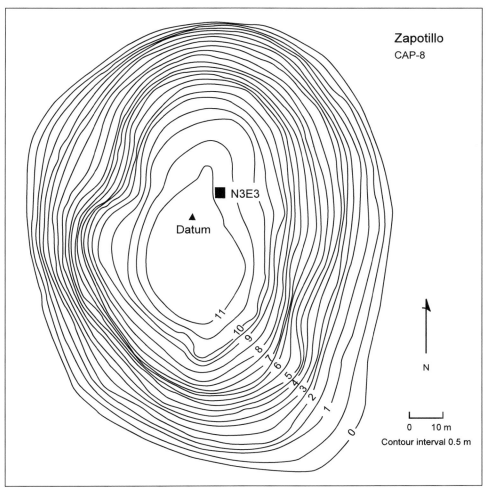

Figure 2.2. Topographic map of the Zapotillo shell mound (map by E. Martínez E.; from Voorhies 2004:Fig. 2.27).

formed rapidly between 2200 and 2700 years BC (Kennett et al. 2007:11) with the deposition of marsh clam shells. Later occupations at the site are difficult to date because the ceramic assemblages from the two excavations are small and the potsherds are in poor condition. Most diagnostic sherds date to the Late Postclassic period, but we also excavated one possible Protoclassic potsherd, and one Middle Preclassic potsherd was collected from the surface (Kennett et al. 2007:6).

Tlacuachero (CAP-7)

Tlacuachero is a shell mound located within the mangrove formation southwest of the embarcadero Las Garzas and west of Laguna Teculapa. The site was first identified and named by Navarrete (personal communication), although it is locally known as Pechón.

The site was mapped, tested, and dated by Voorhies (1976:36 ff; 2004:31-67) who has worked at the site during several field seasons. It is oval in outline and has several low rises on its surface (Figure 2.4) that appear to be platform mounds constructed some time after

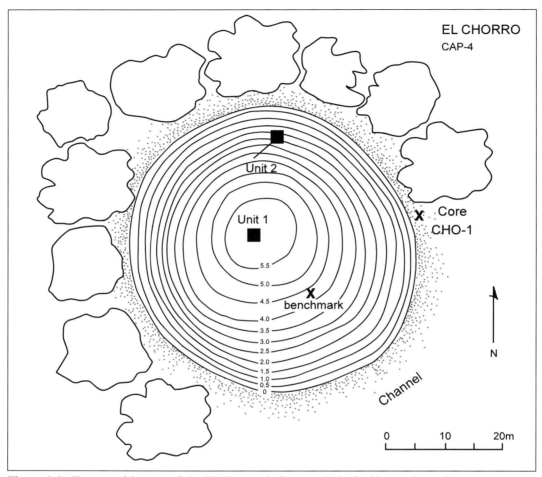

Figure 2.3. Topographic map of the El Chorro shell mound (drafted by A. de Anda).

the Archaic period. The island's area is 2.42 ha[1] and it is over 7 m high. Excavations revealed a Late Archaic period occupation, as well as occupations from the Early through the Late Classic periods. Occupational surfaces dating to the Late Archaic period were discovered in the test pit situated at the highest point of the site. These built clay floors were later investigated by further excavation.

Chantuto (CAP-3)

This shell mound is located at the mouth of the lagoon by the same name. It was discovered by Philip Drucker in 1947 and reported by him in the following year (Drucker 1948).

Drucker did not systematically study the site, but he hastily dug a test pit and discovered an aceramic stratum of shell, which he considered the most significant discovery of the field season (Drucker 1948:165). Lorenzo visited the site in 1953. He dug a second test pit and his results confirmed Drucker's earlier finding (Lorenzo 1955). On the basis of this prior research and that of Voorhies at similar and nearby shell mounds (CAP-4, CAP-6, CAP-7 and CAP-8), it is probable that the core of the Chantuto mound dates to the Late Archaic period. This was confirmed in part by radiocarbon dates from a sediment core that penetrated site deposits (Voorhies 2004:72ff).

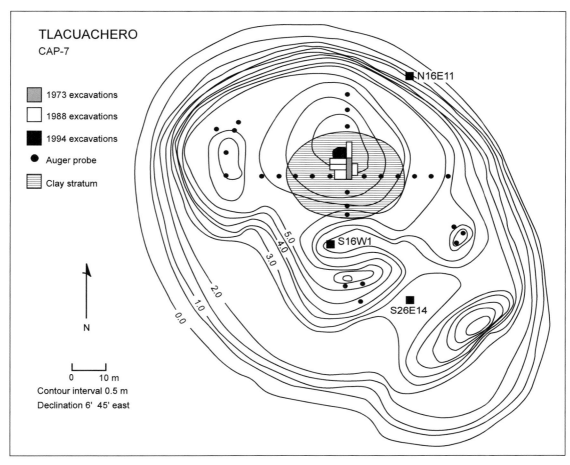

Figure 2.4. Topographic map of the Tlacuachero shell mound (mapped by B. Voorhies, J. Gasco, and G. Michaels; from Voorhies 2004:Fig. 2.3).

The site area is 0.45² ha and it is slightly above 4.5 m in height (Figure 2.5). When we first visited the site it was used as a seasonal camp by local shrimp fishermen and its surface was very disturbed. Abundant marsh clam shells and a few prehistoric sherds were visible on the site surface. Judging from our surface collection of potsherds, the site was occupied during the Protoclassic through Early Classic periods and secondarily in the Late Postclassic period, in addition to the principal occupation during the Archaic period.

EARTHEN MOUNDS

We discovered twelve earthen accumulative mounds in our site survey. As mentioned above only two of these have subsurface investigations.

Los Cerritos (CAP-37)

This site is located on the north shore of the lagoon by the same name. It is a small mound accumulation that measures 0.24 ha and stands over 2.5 m in height. The site is symmetrical in form, with the highest part of the mound at its center (Figure 2.6). At the time of our survey it

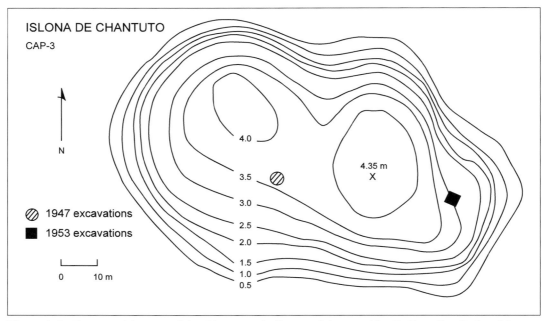

Figure 2.5. Topographic map of the Chantuto shell mound (mapped by F. González Rul and R. Franco S.; adapted by Voorhies [2004:Fig. 2.21] from Lorenzo [1955:no number]).

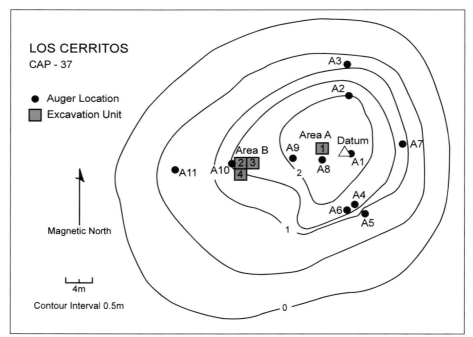

Figure 2.6. Topographic map of the Los Cerritos earthen mound (adapted from Kennett et al. 2002:Fig. 3).

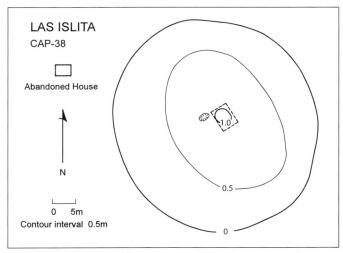

Figure 2.7. Topographic map of La Islita (mapped with compass, tape, and level by J. Mallory; drafted by A. Nethery).

was occupied by fisherfolk of the Los Cerritos fishing cooperative: the survey field crew estimated that approximately 60 houses were present on this small mound at the time it was originally mapped.

Local inhabitants report finding obsidian and figurines as well as potsherds. The survey field crew collected a bag of artifacts and the sherds indicated an occupation spanning the Early through Middle Preclassic periods.

In 2001 Kennett conducted subsurface excavations at Los Cerritos. These consisted of both test pits and auger probes (Kennett et al. 2002). Domestic features, including floors, hearths, and pits, were found in the excavations. The results of these investigations indicate that the site might have been established during the Barra phase (1800-1400 BC), but this is uncertain. It was certainly occupied during the Locona, Ocos, and Cherla phases, all within the Early Preclassic period (Kennett and Voorhies 2001). Radiocarbon dates place the site's principal occupation between 3400 and 3100 cal BP. The excavations did not reveal any Middle Preclassic ceramics as was predicted on the basis of the original study of surface collected sherds.

La Islita (CAP-38)

This mound is located on the northern shore of Laguna Los Cerritos, within the mangrove zone. It is a symmetrical accumulation with the highest point at the center of the island (Figure 2.7). It has no surface features of note other than a small depression near the center of the site that is probably recent. Sherds were found on the site surface, and these provided the dating of the site to the Early and Middle Preclassic periods, with a lighter occupation during the Late Preclassic through Early Classic periods. We also observed marsh clam shells and turtle and crab remains, which could be recent. The site is over a meter in height and has an area of 0.15 ha.

Loma Arturo (CAP-40)

This single mound is located north of Laguna Los Cerritos. It is within the seasonally inundated zone that is used to pasture cattle and is covered in grass. The site surface is disturbed because cattle congregate there, particularly when it rains. This means that artifacts are more abundant than they would be if no surface disturbance was present, and the field crew was able to collect a full bag of sherds. These indicated that the site was occupied during the Early to Middle Preclassic periods, with a

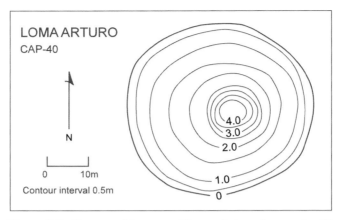

Figure 2.8. Topographic map of Loma Arturo (mapped with compass, tape, and level by J. Mallory; drafted by A. Nethery).

lighter occupation during the Late Preclassic to Early Classic periods.

The site is a circular island that is symmetrical, with the highest point close to the site center (Figure 2.8). Its height is slightly over 4 m and the site area is 0.16 ha. The site is said to be within national territory and was used by the Los Cerritos fishing cooperative at the time of our survey. We named the site after our guide, as at the time of our visit we could not determine what it is called locally.

Isla Tamarindos #2 (CAP-36)

This site is located north of Laguna Los Cerritos but farther inland than the site of Los Cerritos described previously. Isla Tamarindos #2 is situated within the seasonally inundated zone, near the interface between the *madresal* and mangrove formations. The site name derives from the tamarind trees that dominate the vegetation.

The mound is symmetrical, with the highest point at the island center (Figure 2.9). The mound is just over 3 m in height and has an area of 0.26 ha. Surface artifacts were scarce, but a bag of sherds was collected primarily from the back dirt of gopher burrows. The sherds indicate an occupation during the Early to Middle Preclassic and a lighter occupation during the Early Classic period. No marsh clam shells were observed on the surface.

Palo Jiote (CAP-41)

This is a single mound located north of Laguna Los Cerritos and within the mangrove zone. The site is a small (0.0149 ha), symmetrical mound with its highest point (> 1.0 m) at the center (Figure 2.10). There were no faunal remains on the site surface, but sherds were relatively abundant, especially at the mound's edge.

On the basis of the collected sherds, the site was occupied during the Late Preclassic to Early Classic time span.

Isla Belén (MAP-2)

This site is located just west of the Chantuto Lagoon within the seasonally inundated zone. Isla Belén measures 0.0201 ha and stands more than 2.5 m in height (Figure 2.11). The dominant vegetation is *manaca* palm (*Scheelea preussii*), with *piñuela* (*Bromelia karatas* L.) near the shoreline. There are no visible surface features except that the midden accumulation is higher on the northeast side. No shell was found on the surface and only a few eroded sherds were observed. These were low fired and brick red in color. They suggest a Classic period occupation.

El Grillo (CAP-16)

This earthen mound is located east of the Las Garzas embarcadero and north of Laguna Teculapa. It is situated at the interface between

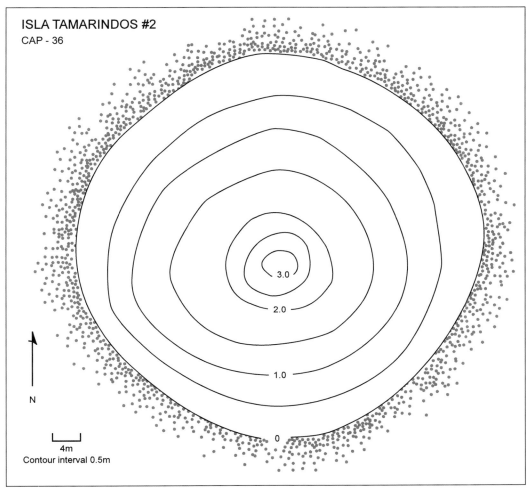

Figure 2.9. Topographic map of Isla Tamarindos 2 (sketch map by J. Mallory; drafted by A. Nethery).

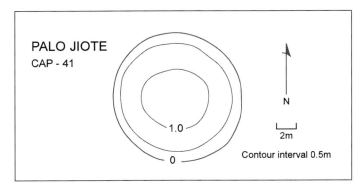

Figure 2.10. Topographic map of Palo Jiote (pace and compass map by B. Voorhies; drafted by A. Nethery).

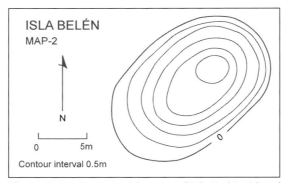

Figure 2.11. Topographic map of Isla Belén (sketch map by B. Voorhies; drafted by A. Nethery).

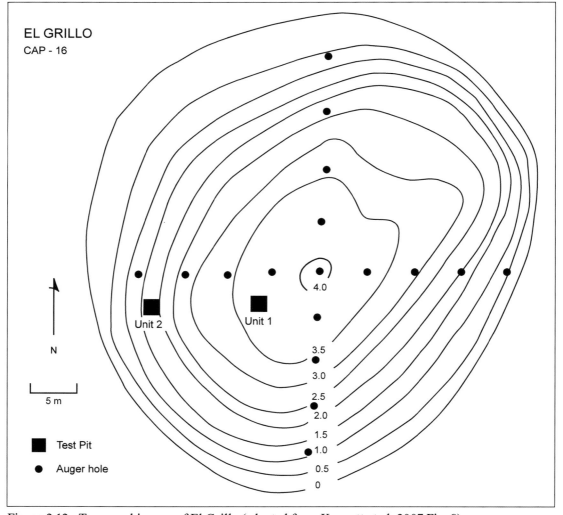

Figure 2.12. Topographic map of El Grillo (adapted from Kennett et al. 2007:Fig. 8).

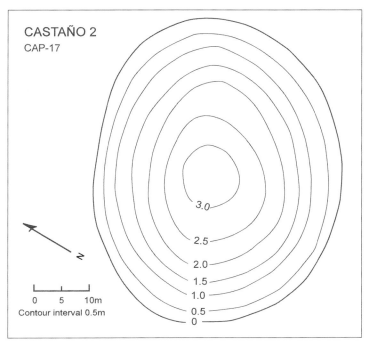

Figure 2.13. Topographic map of Castaño 2 (mapped by J. Gasco and H. Neff; drafted by A. Nethery; from Voorhies and Gasco 2004:Fig. 3.14).

an herbaceous marsh (principally cattails) formation and the mangrove forest formation, only a short distance from the El Chorro shell mound. The site was first discovered and explored in 1978 by the Proyecto Soconusco crew. The island is basically symmetrical, with its highest point (> 4.0 m) near the mound center (Figure 2.12). The island measures 0.2 ha and there are no discernible surface features.

Surface materials observed during the survey included potsherds and marsh clam shells. Both were especially visible near the mound base where burrowing animals bring them to the surface. According to our analysis of the surface sherds, the site was occupied during the Early to Middle Preclassic and Early to Late Classic, with the last occupation being less intense.

In 2005 Kennett investigated the subsurface deposits using auger probes, two excavated test pits, and two sediment cores taken from the bottoms of the test pits (Kennett et al. 2007:13

ff). Evidence of domestic activities recovered from the test pits consisted of living surfaces, perhaps floors, trash deposits, pits and burned areas that could be hearths. Radiocarbon dates span 1500 to 1150 BC, which coincides nicely with the ceramic study that indicates people were on site during the Locona-Ocos, Cherla, and Cuadros phases of the Early Preclassic period (Kennett et al. 2007:25). According to our data, a small settled community was established at this site during the Locona Phase (ca. 1400 BC) and lasted until the end of the Cuadros phase (ca. 1150 BC; Kennett et al. 2007:26).

Castaño #2 (CAP-17)

Castaño #2 is located north of Laguna Los Cerritos. It was discovered on the basis of photo imagery and ground verified by us during the first season of Proyecto Soconusco. It is a symmetrically shaped mound, oval in outline, with the highest point (> 3.0 m) at its center (Figure 2.13). The area of the island is 0.2 ha.

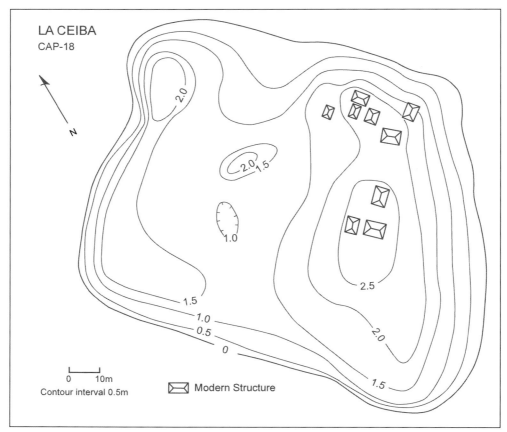

Figure 2.14. Topographic map of La Ceiba (mapped by J. Gasco and H. Neff; drafted A. Nethery).

The site is surrounded by mangrove forest and supports deciduous vegetation that is typical of this area.

Sherds and shell were collected from the site surface. Both marsh clams (*Polymesoda radiata*) and ark (*Anadara* sp.) shells were found. The site was occupied during the Early-Middle Preclassic and again possibly during the Late Postclassic period, based upon an analysis of surface sherds.

La Ceiba (CAP-18)

La Ceiba is a mound located within the herbaceous swamp formation north of Laguna Teculapa and east of Laguna Los Cerritos. It is situated at the mouth of Río Teculapa. It

was first detected from photo imagery and ground verified by us during the initial season of Proyecto Soconusco. This site is somewhat rectangular in outline (Figure 2.14). Platform mounds are present, which distinguish this site from many, but not all of the mounds discussed here. The site area is 0.98 ha, and its highest point is on the eastern side.

Surface collected pottery suggests that it was occupied continuously from the Early Preclassic through Middle Classic periods. We conjecture that the platform mounds date to the Classic occupation of the site, but this has not been confirmed. A few Late Postclassic period sherds suggest to us that a light occupation occurred at that time as well.

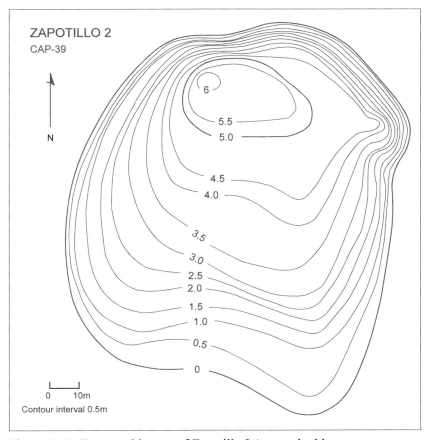

Figure 2.15. Topographic map of Zapotillo 2 (mapped with compass, tape, and level by A. Gerstle).

Zapotillo #2 (CAP-39)

This island site is west of Laguna Los Cerritos, at the interface between the mangrove and madresal formations. The site is slightly rectangular in outline with its highest elevation (> 6 m) at the north end (Figure 2.15). Several low rises may be platform mounds, but these are difficult to distinguish clearly. At the time of our survey the site was used for agriculture, especially for palm and plantains.

Some marsh clam shell was seen on the site surface and potsherds were collected. We identified a continuous occupation from the Early Preclassic through the Late Classic periods with some Late Postclassic period sherds also present.

Isla Tamarindos #1 (CAP-33)

This mound is located north of Laguna Los Cerritos, on the interface between the mangrove and madresal formations. The site plan is kidney-shaped, with its highest elevation (> 5.0 m) toward the southern end of the island (Figure 2.16). It is 0.46 ha in area, with two platform mounds visible on the site surface.

Surface materials include marsh clams and other ecofacts, as well as pottery, Acacoyagua I figurines (cf. Drucker 1948: Figure 7), and obsidian. Based on our analysis of this pottery, the site was occupied throughout the prehistoric period, with the exception of the poorly documented Early Postclassic, with the heaviest occupation during the Early to Middle Preclassic periods.

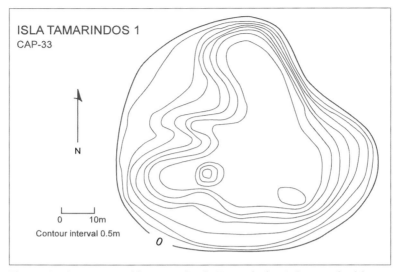

Figure 2.16. Topographic map of Isla Tamarindos 1 (mapped with compass, tape, and level by J. Mallory and B. Voorhies).

Isla Cigueña (MAP-3)

A short distance from MAP-2 is another site called Isla Cigueña. The two sites are very similar and probably have similar histories. Isla Cigueña is a single mound accumulation that forms an island within the wetlands. *Manaca* palms are the dominant vegetation and *piñuela* fringes the shore. The site is over 2.5 m in height and has an area of 0.0287 ha (Figure 2.17). Like the nearby site, there are no surface features other than the fact that the mound is higher on the northeast side. Only a few nondiagnostic sherds were collected from the site surface and no shell was observed. The site is undated.

SPATIAL PATTERNS

As may be seen in Figure 1.2, all the accumulative mounds are situated close to and along the inland boundary of the mangrove formation. Almost all of these sites are either surrounded by water or, if not within the littoral zone proper, they are spatially close to its inland margin. The circular outlines of these accumulative sites suggest to us that they all formed as islands within the wetlands (Waselkov 1987), since debris accumulation would not be constrained to a single location if it took place on dry land. In two instances (the El Chorro shell mound and the El Grillo earthen mound), sediment core probes demonstrated that the mounds were originally formed on a substrate of mangrove mud. All these sites have early occupations, dating initially from the Late Archaic period in the case of the shell mounds, and from the Early Preclassic period in the case of the two studied earthen mounds. By extension, the other earthen mounds probably began to be formed during the Preclassic period, but this is conjecture and needs verification.

It is likely that the shell mounds formed initially near the edges of lagoons where the focal marsh clam resource was concentrated. Undoubtedly, the clams were collected during low tides and brought back to a processing location that was conveniently close to the resource patch. Because it was necessary to cook the clams in order to open the shells and extract the meat, the human foragers needed dry land where they could carry out their clambakes. It is likely that during the Late Archaic period only the gradually accumulating artificial islands provided the requisite conditions. That is, we suspect that the inactive barrier beaches

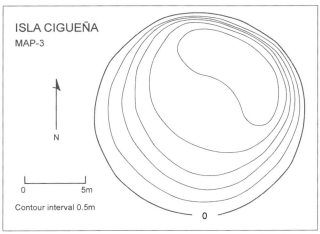

Figure 2.17. Topographic map of Isla Cigueña (sketch map by B. Voorhies; drafted by A. Nethery).

that are located seaward of the shell mounds had not yet been formed when the shell mounds were first accumulating.

The earthen mounds also most likely were initially formed within the wetlands, but most are situated now within the seasonally inundated biotic zone, located just inland of the present day wetlands. Paleoenvironmental studies of the sediments adjacent to these mounds have been conducted only at El Grillo (Core GRI-1), but the circular outlines of all these sites suggest that they accumulated within a wet environment.

At present, we know a lot more about the processes of site formation and inferences about human behavior for the shell mounds than we do about the earthen mounds. Voorhies (2004) has argued that during the Late Archaic period the people responsible for the formation of the shell mounds were logistically mobile foragers who were moving regularly between inland residential bases and the shell mounds of the wetlands. She interprets the shell mounds as processing locations for lagoonal resources including marsh clams, fish, and most probably shrimp.

Limited excavations have been carried out at only two earthen mound sites. What is clear from the currently available data is that some features archaeologists consider to be indicators of residential sedentism are present in the earthen mound sites, whereas they are notably absent in the shell mounds. These include burned areas, possibly hearths, pits, floors, and trash deposits. These features are reiterative in the small excavations at two earthen mound sites, so we can be confident that there was much more residential permanency in the wetlands when the earthen mounds were accumulating compared with earlier. Paleobotanical indicators of farming also increase in the earthen mounds compared with the shell mounds. Accordingly, we are confident that we can detect the settlement and subsistence changes as the coastal population was transitioning economically away from fished, collected, and hunted foods toward a greater dependency upon farming.

ENDNOTES

1   The area of Tlacuachero was previously reported incorrectly as 1.41 ha (Voorhies 2004:Table 2.1).

2   The area of Chantuto was previously reported incorrectly as 0.61 ha (Voorhies 2004:Table 2.1).

CHAPTER 3

SITES WITH FINAL, EARLY CLASSIC PERIOD OCCUPATIONS

In this chapter we discuss the archaeological sites in our inventory that were last occupied in the Early Classic period, after which they were effectively abandoned. As we mentioned in Chapter 1, we are interested in investigating the site plans for individual time periods in order to identify patterned regularities, if any, that might shed light on the sociopolitical organization of the site users for that time interval. Although our investigations enabled us to identify many sites that were built between the time of the initial appearance of earthen mounds and the Early Classic period, all those sites continued to be occupied during later periods. This means that the earlier architectural layouts likely are obscured by later construction episodes and that they are unavailable to us without major excavations at multiple sites. In view of the fact that such excavations have not been undertaken, the Early Classic period is the next chronological period for which we are able to address the question of intrasite settlement patterns.

Even when we attempt to discern intrasite patterns pertaining to the Early Classic period, the task is difficult because so many of the sites that were occupied at that time continued to be occupied in the Late Classic period. In fact, only fourteen sites were effectively abandoned at the end of the Early Classic period, although 80 sites were occupied during that period (Figure 3.1). This means that our sample of Early Classic period sites to be examined for patterns in settlement layout represents only 17.5 percent of the sites occupied during that time period. Such a low percentage means that any generalities offered must be considered only as working hypotheses.

SITE DESCRIPTIONS

The fourteen sites with terminal Early Classic occupations are discussed below. They range from sites with only a single low platform mound to sites with multiple platform mounds and several mound types.

Tepalcatenco (CAC-1)

When we first visited this site in 1978, it was located on the outskirts of the town Acacoyagua where people lived in modest houses among their cacao orchards. Drucker (1948:161) originally discussed this site, which he called Acacoyagua. He had seen a collection of figurines belonging to the botanist Dr. Eizi Matuda who directed Drucker to their place of origin. Drucker dug three trenches at the site and recovered figurines, fragments of ceramic vessels, and some stone tools (Drucker n.d.).

Since Drucker's time Tepalcatenco has been looted to some extent, as figurines from the site are now abundant in the archaeological collections of local inhabitants. Still, we observed no major damage due to looting activities during our investigations, and most of the collected archaeological materials were probably found during house and well construction rather than from intentional looting at the site.

This site is located in the foothills of the Sierra Madre where the terrain is moderately hilly. The larger mounds of the site are situated on a smooth, gently sloping hillside (Figure 3.2). The tallest mound at the site is located on this slope at a higher elevation relative to the other mounds. It stands 4.5 m above the adjacent ground level but appears more monumental due to its hilltop position. There are four mounds close to the base of this conical mound situated on the downslope side. In general the mounds at the site are not arranged around plazas, and we detect no particular regularity in the site layout. There are 30 mounds within an area of 14.99 ha.

The site was occupied over a long period of time, but the major period of activity dates from the Late Preclassic through the Early Classic periods. Less intense occupations are indicated,

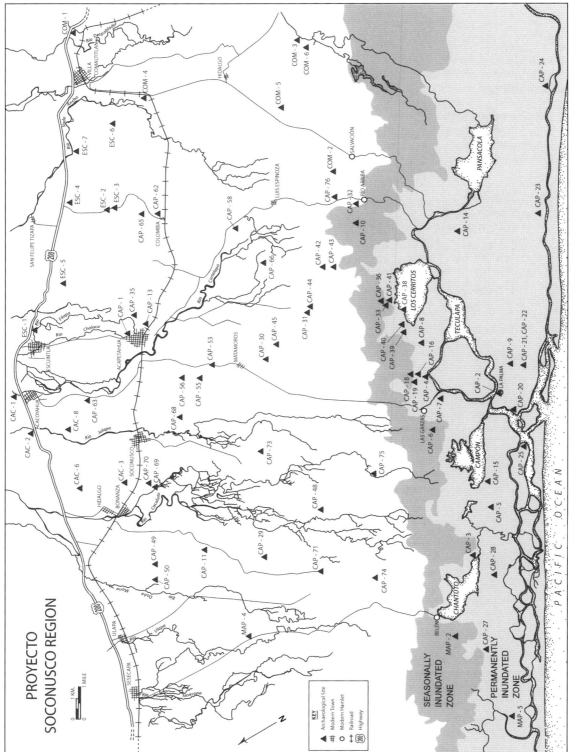

Figure 3.1. Archaeological sites occupied during the Early Classic period (from Voorhies 1989b:Fig. 5.12).

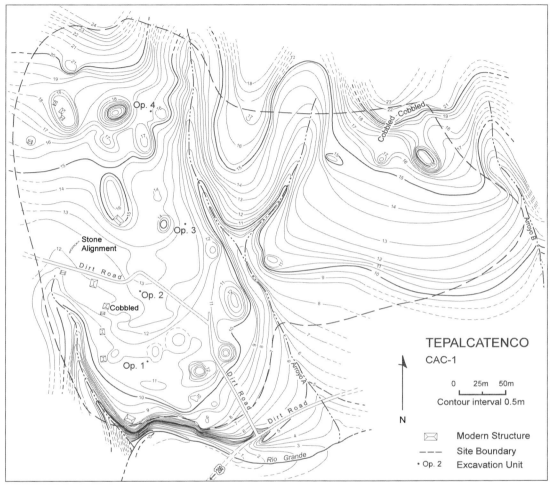

Figure 3.2. Topographic map of Tepalcatenco (mapped by J. Gasco, L. Pfeiffer, and D. Hosler; drafted by A. Nethery; from Voorhies and Gasco 2004: Fig. 3.15).

beginning from the Early Preclassic period and lasting through the Late Classic period. Also, our analysis of sherds collected from the surface suggests that the site had a light Late Postclassic period occupation, which was confirmed by material recovered from several test pits. Our justification for including this site in the present chapter is that we think the settlement layout dates to the Early Classic period and that during the Late Postclassic period no major construction was undertaken.

We excavated four test pits located along the hill slope that has the majority of mounds upon it. These excavations will be discussed below.

Operation 1. This operation, excavated by Field Assistant James M. Kules, was the closest of the four test pits to the Río Grande, a small stream at the base of the hill. The test pit was situated on flat ground near the edge of a platform mound cluster. The test pit measured 1.5 m by 1.5 m and was dug to a depth of 1.45 m. An auger probe to 1.65 m confirmed that the base of the cultural deposits had been reached at the bottom of our excavation. As may be seen in the profile (Figure 3.3) there are several distinct soil types, two middens, and five pits that were located near the bottom of the excavation. Despite the differences in stratigraphy, analysis

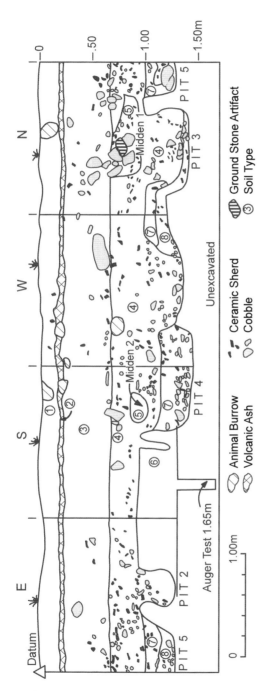

Figure 3.3. Stratigraphic profile of Op. 1, Tepalcatenco (see soil descriptions in Table 3.1).

of the ceramics revealed that all the different stratigraphic events occurred within the same broadly defined period that falls within the Protoclassic to Early Classic periods.

The test pit probed primary undisturbed deposits. Most features, such as midden deposits and pits, were undisturbed. Also, many artifacts were found just as they had been discarded, with broken fragments close together. We speculate that the test pit may have been in the ancient yard of a household complex. An alignment of rocks, encountered in the northwest corner of the pit at 0.50-0.60 m, is probably a wall foundation but our excavations exposed only a very short section of the feature. Domestic rubbish, mainly broken grinding tools and smashed pots, are associated with this alignment. For example, a large waterworn boulder fragment with an area smoothed by grinding (FN #5085), and a boulder whetstone (FN #5086) were found. Midden 1 probably is contemporaneous with the alignment since it was dug into Soil 4, the upper contact of which supports the base of the stone alignment. This midden contained rich organic soil, broken tools (percussor fragment FN #5092 and mano fragment FN #5086), and other rocks.

Midden 2 is located at a lower level than Midden 1 and is not clearly associated with any other feature. It is under a large rock embedded in the south wall of the excavation and contains a dense concentration of sherds and figurine fragments (Figure 3.4). Some of the figurine fragments were lost because we unwisely left them partially excavated overnight and they were stolen by the next morning.

At approximately the 1.0 m level the openings of some of the five refuse pits began to appear. These were dug into a sterile stratum, Soil 6. Pit 1, contained no noteworthy objects, only broken rocks and sherds. One adobe fragment apparently from a prepared surface was recovered from the 1.10-1.30 m level of this pit. Pit 2 contained figurine fragments and some obsidian, as well as many cracked rocks, some of which may have come from grinding stones. Pit 3 also contained figurine fragments, charcoal, broken rocks and other debris. Pits 4 and 5 had contents that were similar in nature to those of the other refuse pits.

Table 3.1. Soil descriptions pertaining to stratigraphic profiles of excavation units of Tepalcatenco (CAC-1).

Operation 1 (see Figure 3.3)

Soil number	Descriptions
1	Brown-dark brown sandy silt (10YR 4/3)
2	Volcanic ash (10YR 5/2)
3	Dark brown silty clay (10YR 3/2)
4	Very dark grayish brown silty clay (10YR 3/2)
5	Brown-black clay (10YR 4/8)
6	Reddish sandy clay, sterile (10YR 4/8)
7	Red-brown clay (10YR 3/3)
8	Brown-black clay with abundant charcoal

Operation 2 (see Figure 3.5)

1	Dark brown sandy silt (10YR 5/3)
2	Dark brown clay (10YR 3/3)
3	Light brown sandy silt (10YR 5/6)
4	Yellow brown coarse sandy silt (10YR 5/6)
5	Dark brown sandy silt with charcoal and adobe fragments (5YR 5/2)
6	Reddish sandy clay with decomposing rocks, sterile (7.5YR 5/8)
7	Yellow brown sand (10YR 6/4)
8	Dark brown silty clay (10YR 2.5/1)

Operation 3, Unit 1 (see Figure 3.7)

1	Gray, friable silty clay topsoil (10YR 4/2)
2	Orange-tan silty alluvial clay (10YR 4/3)
3	Sandy clay with granodiorite gravel (10YR 5/3)
4	Yellow-orange sandy clay grading into sterile (10YR 5/6)

Operation 2. This test pit is located due north and upslope from Operation 1 and is situated on flat ground between two large platform mounds. Field Assistant Ann Bennett excavated the unit that measured 1.5 m by 1.5 m. It was excavated to sterile soil at a depth of 1.45 m (Figure 3.5).

This test pit revealed a situation that is generally similar to that of Operation 1. Rock alignments suggest the presence of wall foundations, and refuse pits were dug into the sterile soil at the bottom of the excavations. Also, abundant domestic refuse was found throughout the pit.

The upper 30 cm of the excavation contained mixed cultural material that is Protoclassic and Late Postclassic in age. There is stratigraphic evidence of much physical disturbance due to roots and rodents in these upper 30 cm. The upper 10 cm contained recent material such as metal, glass, and plastic, as well as a glass marble. The volcanic ash layer

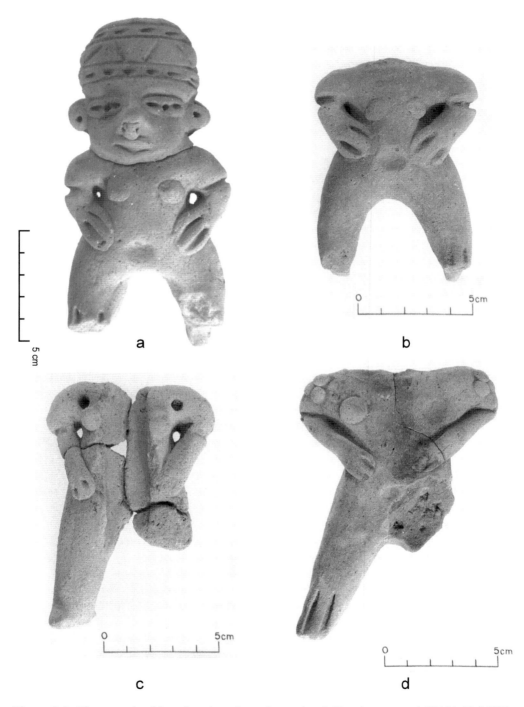

Figure 3.4. Photograph of four figurines from Operation 1, Tepalcatenco: a) #5091; b) #5978; c) #5979; d) #5980.

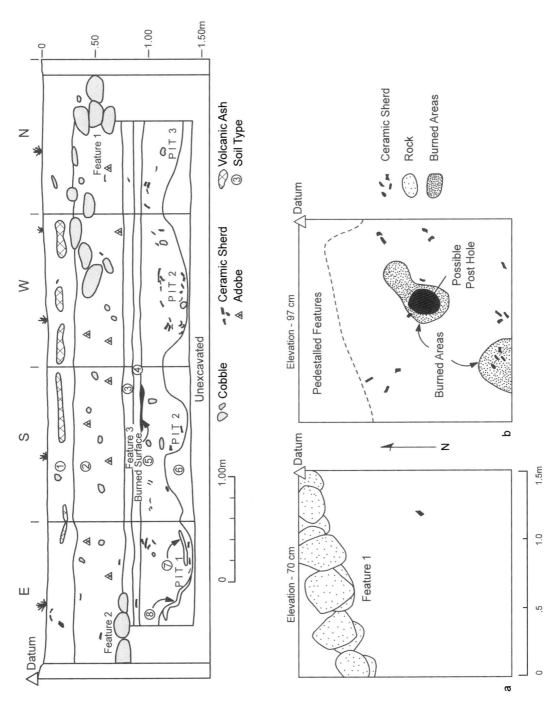

Figure 3.5. Stratigraphic profile of Op. 2, Tepalcatenco (see soil descriptions in Table 3.1).

Figure 3.6. Plan views from Op. 2, Tepalcatenco: a) Feature 1; b) Post hole and burned areas.

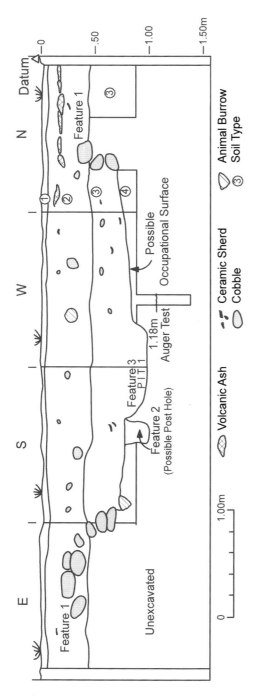

Figure 3.7. Stratigraphic profile of Op. 3, Tepalcatenco (see soil descriptions in Table 3.1).

begins at approximately 10 cm, but it is patchy in this unit. The contact between soils 1 and 2 is at the 30 cm level. The top of a rock wall was encountered at this same level in the northern portion of the test pit. This was designated Feature 1 (Figure 3.6a). It has three courses of boulders, and its strike was north 75 degrees east. Several of its stones were reused artifacts. The bottom of the feature was at 0.70 m.

A second alignment, Feature 2, was directly beneath Feature 1 and perpendicular to it. It was only one course high and rested directly upon and within Soil 3. The soil and the feature must have been deposited simultaneously. At 0.90 m a flat, thin stratum, Soil 4, was discovered. It contained only a few small artifacts and might have been a living surface such as a floor or house yard. Under the lower contact of Soil 4, near the center of the test pit, a burned area appears to mark the former location of a post (Figure 3.6b). In the center of the burned area there is a circular area that is unburned. The burned soil forms a ring around this circle and extends approximately 30 cm in one direction. Presumably a burning post that collapsed to the northeast created this feature. The hole was traced with some difficulty to 1.22 m. A second patch of burned soil was found at the same level near the south wall of the test pit. The only interpretation we have of this is that most of a previous prepared surface has been removed by erosion, with only two isolated patches remaining. The two stone alignments and the possible prepared surface are Protoclassic in age. Only Protoclassic material was recovered in this test pit between the 0.30 and 1.15 m levels.

Underlying the burned areas, designated as Feature 3, is the upper contact of Soil 5, a dark brown, organic rich stratum. This soil contained dense quantities of sherds, broken rocks, charcoal, adobe fragments, and obsidian debitage. It is clearly a midden deposit. A charcoal sample was collected from Soil 5 at 1.15 m. It was radiocarbon dated at 2220 +/- 120 years ago. The lower contact of Soil 5 is very irregular because three pits, filled with the midden, had been dug into the underlying Soil 6. We found charcoal, abundant sherds, figurine fragments and obsidian in all the pits. Soil 6 is

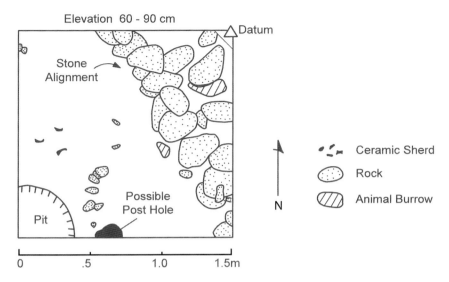

Figure 3.8. Plan view of stone alignment, Op. 3, Tepalcatenco.

the same sterile soil encountered at the bottom of Operation 1.

Operation 3. This 1.5 by 1.5 m excavation was placed on flat terrain farther uphill from Operation 2, and due east of a low mound. Field Assistant John Carpenter directed the excavation. Our expectation was that the pit would penetrate horizontally stratified deposits, as was the case in the first two operations. Contrary to this, the excavation encountered a substantial retaining wall constructed of boulders that consisted of 4-5 courses (Figure 3.7). Furthermore, the wall sloped in such a way that we think it faced west, rather than east, as would be expected if it had served as a terrace edging the down slope side of a plaza. In other words, the excavation apparently revealed a portion of a platform mound that was entirely covered by post constructional sediments.

The strike of the wall is 150 degrees, and it has a maximum height of 0.70 m (Figure 3.8). One boulder (FN #5392) with curvilinear grooves, which may be either a sculpture or a whetsone, was incorporated into the highest course. We did not find any traces of clay plaster on the wall surface or near it.

After the test pit had been dug to sterile soil, and we formulated the hypothesis that it

was a west-facing wall, it became apparent that we did not have the data necessary to date the feature. This is because the excavations were mainly in the postconstructional sediment that had accumulated near the platform after its abandonment. Except for the upper 0.20 m where Late Postclassic material was mixed with Protoclassic to Early Classic material, all the diagnostic material at lower levels dated to the earlier time span, i.e., the Protoclassic. These were secondary deposits and did not directly date the structure.

In order to address the question of dating we opened another 1.5 by 1.5 m unit due east of the first test pit. According to our thinking this unit would have entered the fill of the buried platform. When this area was excavated no characteristic platform fill was found but rather the soils were similar to those found on the other side of the feature. This does not support the platform hypothesis but neither does it refute it conclusively. Except for the upper 0.15 m where mixing with Late Postclassic material was present, the other levels had only Protoclassic to Early Classic material.

A possible occupation surface was found extending away from the feature in the first unit. This is also the upper contact of Soil 4, but Carpenter noted that the lowest course of the wall rests perfectly on this surface. Soil 4 is sterile. Two pits were dug into this stratum and contained the same Soil 3 that overlies Soil 4. Unlike the pits excavated in operations 1 and 2, these pits contained no evidence of trash accumulations but were remarkably free of artifacts.

Operation 4. This 1.5 by 1.5 m test pit was placed east of the highest mound at the site in a clear, flat area between the high mound and one of the small mounds near its base. Field assistant Clare Yarborough excavated the test pit. We had hoped to find a prepared floor that could be dated in order to ascertain the date of the complex. Unfortunately, no prepared surface was encountered. Rather, about 0.40 m of slope wash underlay the humus layer and this, in turn, was underlain by the sterile B horizon soil. As might be expected, relatively few artifacts were recovered from this pit, and most of the sherds were weathered. The pit was dug to 0.95 m and probed an additional meter, but no change in soil was encountered.

In short, this pit produced very little information. All diagnostic sherds were from the Protoclassic time span, which implies that the temple platform dates to the same time. This is because the slope wash must have derived in large part from the highest mound. The only other observation of significance is that several globules of an organic substance, possibly resin, were found in the pit. We think that this substance may have been used in ceremonies on the adjacent platform. This would support the idea that the tall, conical mound was a temple platform.

Amatillo (CAP-28)

Amatillo is located within the wetlands on an inactive beach ridge south of Laguna Chantuto. This beach ridge is a continuation of the landform on which the sites Apazotal, Herrado, and Campito are located. The site was discovered during the 1978-1979 field season of Proyecto Soconusco.

The appearance of Amatillo (Figure 3.9), like its situation, strongly resembles that of

Apazotal (see below). Amatillo consists of two mounds, one of which is 1.5 m in height above the adjacent ground level. The other mound is barely perceptible.

At the time the survey crew visited the site it was densely covered in secondary growth, thus making mapping and artifact collection especially difficult. The site should be investigated during the dry season when visibility might be better. The apparent size of the site is 0.35 ha.

The site was occupied from the Late Preclassic through the Early Classic periods, according to our analysis of surface collected potsherds.

Lomas San Francisco (CAP-48)

The site we call Lomas San Francisco is located southwest of Bonanza in the lower gradient of the coastal plain where flooding occurs seasonally. It is a small site (0.23 ha) with only two mounds (Figure 3.10). One of these is 2.5 m high, whereas the other is less than a half a meter in height. Only a few sherds were collected, but the site appears to have been occupied from the Late Preclassic through the Early Classic periods.

Lomas San Juan (CAP-49)

This site is located approximately 2 km west of Bonanza. It is close to the foothills but is situated on flat terrain. The site is very small, consisting of two low mounds in an area of 0.26 ha (Figure 3.11). The highest mound is only 1 m above the surrounding land surface. Judging from their appearance, the mounds may have been used for residential rather than public functions.

Only a very few ceramics were recovered from the site surface, but these were dated to the Late Preclassic through the Early Classic periods.

Zorrillo (CAP-62)

Zorrillo is located just north of the *colonia* with the same name (also known as Ejido Colombia) and near the railroad line. It is situated on a low knoll about 0.5 km from

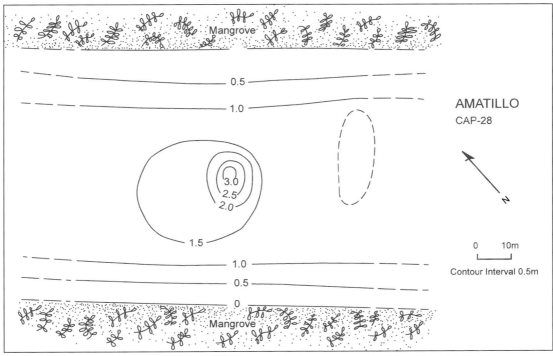

Figure 3.9. Topographic map of Amatillo (mapped by J. Gasco and B. Voorhies; drafted by A. Nethery).

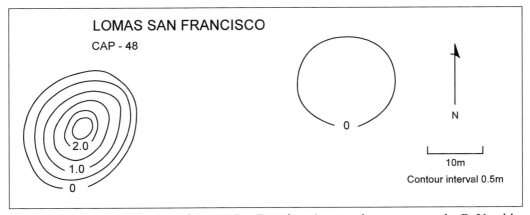

Figure 3.10. Topographic map of Lomas San Francisco (pace and compass map by B. Voorhies; drafted by A. Nethery).

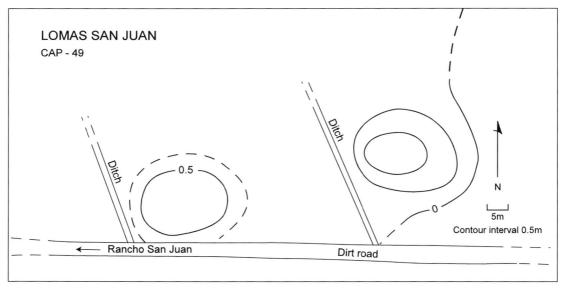

Figure 3.11. Topographic map of Lomas San Juan (sketch map by A. Gerstle; drafted by A. Nethery).

the lowest foothills. It has been disturbed to a limited degree by looting. The site consists of 17 platform mounds in an area of 3.57 ha (Figure 3.12). The larger, apparently public mounds of the site form two rows, with an oblong platform closing the south end of the intervening corridor. Six small, low mounds are adjacent to this complex. There are two tall mounds that are probably temple platforms, or at least platforms for small buildings that were not residential. The higher of the two mounds is 5.0 m above the adjacent ground level.

The site has been dated from the Late Preclassic through the Early Classic periods on the basis of surface-collected sherds.

Rancho Ancheta (ESC-4)

Rancho Ancheta is located near the intersection of the road leading to Ejido Colombia (Zorrillo) from Route 200. It consists of three mounds situated on slightly rolling terrain and a depression that may be a borrow pit. All mounds are small and low and may have been residential in function (Figure 3.13), but they do not form a distinct plaza group. The site area is 0.26 ha and the highest mound is only 0.5 m in elevation.

The site dates to the Late Preclassic through Early Classic periods based upon the surface-collected potsherds.

Lomas Flor (ESC-5)

Lomas Flor is situated on a flat ridge top surrounded by arroyos, approximately 0.5 km south of Route 200 and two km southeast of Escuintla. It was found during the survey of Transect G-23 (Figure 1.21). It consists of two mounds in an area of 0.15 ha (Figure 3.14). The higher mound is a meter in elevation. Both mounds may have been residential in function.

The site has been dated from the Late Preclassic through the Early Classic periods.

Loma José (ESC-6)

Loma José is located west of Villa Comaltitlán on Transect G-28 (Figure 1.22). The terrain is flat but very close to the base of the foothills. The single mound is a meter high and the site area is 0.01 ha (Figure 3.15). Apparently this is a residential mound.

The site dates to the Late Preclassic through Early Classic periods.

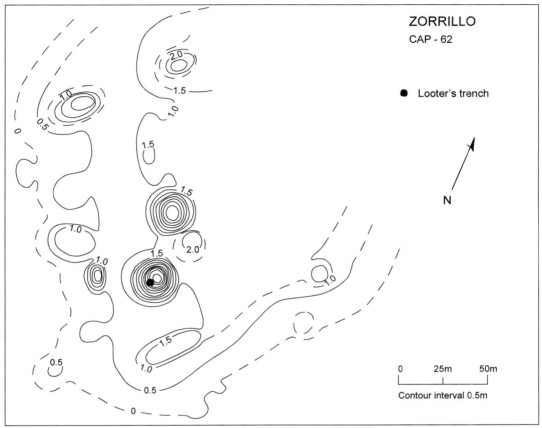

Figure 3.12. Topographic map of Zorrillo (sketch map by S. Levy and J. Mallory; drafted by A. Nethery).

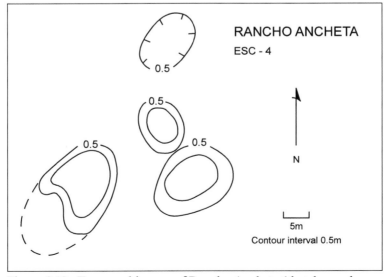

Figure 3.13. Topographic map of Rancho Ancheta (sketch map by S. Levy and J. Mallory; drafted by A. Nethery).

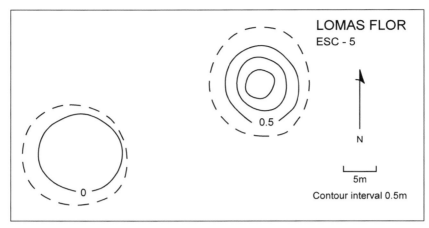

Figure 3.14. Topographic map of Lomas Flor (sketch map by M. Jaffe; drafted by A. Nethery).

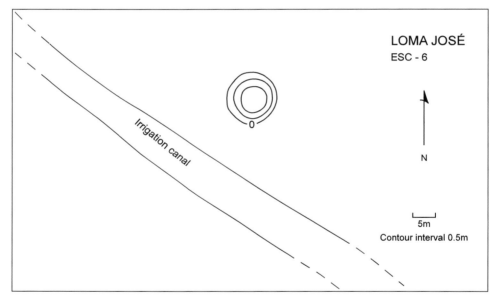

Figure 3.15. Topographic map of Loma José (sketch map by A. Gerstle; drafted by A. Nethery).

Panteón (ESC-1)

The site of Panteón is located in part within the Escuintla town cemetery and lies adjacent to highway Route 200, east of the town. In this location the topography consists of low, rolling hills typical of the lowest portion of the piedmont. Arroyos bound the site on the east and south, but these carry water only during the rainy season. This does not seem to be the same Escuintla site reported by Culebro (1939:37; cited in Piña Chan 1967:61) since he mentions scattered mounds within the town itself. Drucker (n.d.:63, 1948) reports that he observed sherds eroding from a gully near the Escuintla cemetery. Judging from the description, this could be the same gully shown in the southeast corner of the site map. Local children dig figurines from the sidewalls of the gully at

Figure 3.16. Photograph of donated figurine head from Panteón. Head is 4 cm high.

the present time. One such figurine that was presented to Voorhies shows Olmec influence (Figure 3.16).

The site, which is very disturbed due to activities within the cemetery, measures 10.65 ha. We identified 14 mounds within this area. Several of these mounds appear to have cobble retaining walls, but no plaza groups have been identified (Figure 3.17), and we detect no particular pattern in the distribution of mounds. The highest mound is 3.5 m and is situated on the highest point of the site. Stone alignments were observed on the road that bisects the site; we are uncertain whether these are prehistoric or modern features. Informants say that they were constructed recently to provide traction for wheeled vehicles, but some seem to extend beyond the limits of the road. They may be foundation stones for houses but this is not certain.

The site was occupied from the Late Preclassic through the Late Classic periods with the major occupation during the Late Preclassic through the Early Classic periods. Despite the evidence for an occupation during the Late Classic period we include this site here on the basis of the apparently heavier occupation during the Early Classic period.

Los Carlos (COM-1)

The site of Los Carlos is located on Finca Los Carlos and is bisected by Route 200. It is situated in the low rolling hills of the piedmont and extends close to the east bank of the Río Despoblado. We discovered it during the 1978-1979 field season of Proyecto Soconusco, but we learned later that Carlos Navarrete marked its location on his unpublished map of coastal Chiapas. Apparently, Navarrete did not actually visit the site since it was not named. We considered Los Carlos the most attractive site discovered during the first field season because of its undulating topography and the lush grass that cloaks the platforms. The site is maintained as a pasture for cattle. Even thirty years later the site remains virtually undisturbed.

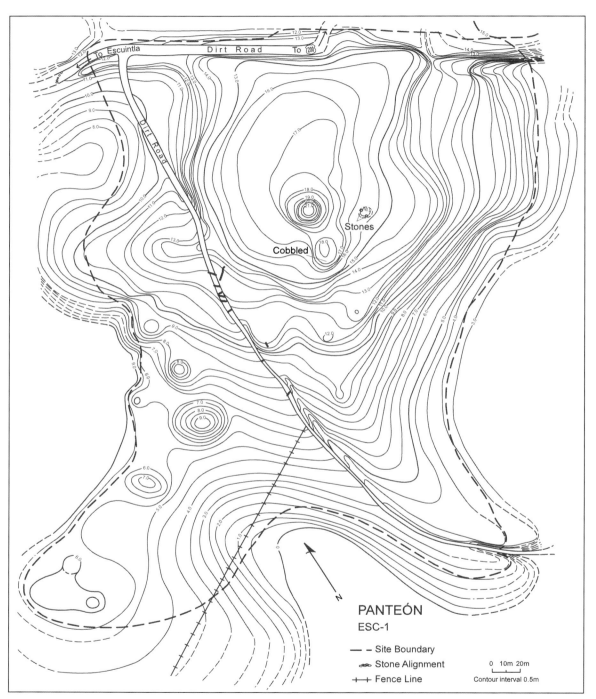

Figure 3.17. Topographic map of Panteón (mapped by J. Gasco, D. Hosler, and L. Pfeiffer; drafted by A. Nethery).

The site covers 10.79 ha within which 27 mounds have been recorded (Figure 3.18). The highest mound is located on the eastern periphery of the site and is 10.5 m above the adjacent ground level. It is located on top of a hill and must have been particularly imposing when in use. Cobbles eroding from the fill indicate that it, as well as other mounds at the site, was rock faced. The remaining mounds are located to the west and across the modern highway from this dominant construction. Seven platform mounds are arranged so that they form a plaza complex that is open on the west side. In this study, we are reserving the term "plaza" to refer to architectural groups such as this one where there is an open area delimited by mounds laid out in alignments. Despite the considerable amount of construction, the formal planning, and the site accessibility we did not find a ball court.

The site occupation spanned the Late Preclassic through the Late Classic periods, with the Late Preclassic to Early Classic interval being represented by the largest number of potsherds.

Rancho Marfil (COM-4)

Rancho Marfil is located just east of the Río Vado Ancho next to the railroad line that passes between the towns of Acapetahua and Villa Comaltitlán. The site covers 2.32 ha and contains eight mounds (Figure 3.19). Several mounds are as high as 1.0 m, but the rest of the mounds are only 0.5 m high. A stone alignment was clearly observed alongside one mound. Rancho Marfil was occupied mainly in the Late Preclassic through the Early Classic periods, but a secondary occupation continued throughout the Late Classic. We detected no formal architectural pattern at this site.

Apazotal (CAP-27)

Apazotal is located within the mangroves on an island west of Laguna Chantuto. The island is part of the long, linear inactive beach ridge that affords the most significant extension of dry land in the wetlands of the study area. A narrow waterway, Lagartero, separates this piece of land

from the rest of the inactive beach to the east, known as Cocal. We discovered the site during the first season of Proyecto Soconusco.

The site consists of two small coalescing mounds, the higher of which is now 2.5 m above the adjacent ground level (Figure 3.20). Although we tried hard to find other mounds or surface artifacts away from the mounds, nothing else was discovered. The size of the site is approximately 0.25 ha. The site was occupied from the Late Preclassic through the Early Classic periods, with a less intense occupation during the Late Postclassic period.

Loma Sandía (CAP-70)

This is a single, rather large mound that is only a meter high (Figure 3.21). It is situated on flat terrain about 2 km south of Bonanza. The site area is 0.10 ha.

The site dates from the Protoclassic through the Early Classic periods.

Vado Ancho (ESC-7)

Vado Ancho was discovered during the survey of Transect G-28 (Figure 1.22). It is located on the west bank of the Río Vado Ancho near Route 200. The site consists of six mounds in an area of 0.54 ha (Figure 3.22) and is situated upon a low hill. The large mound to the south has an exposure of boulders that are laid in stepped courses. From the site layout one can conjecture that it represents a residential complex, but this has not been tested by subsurface investigations. The highest mound is now 1.5 m in height. We detected no formal site planning.

The site dates from the Protoclassic through the Early Classic periods.

INTRASITE SETTLEMENT PATTERNS AND BURIAL PATTERNS

As we mentioned at the beginning of the chapter many of the sites in our inventory were occupied during the Early Classic period. In fact, this time period has the greatest number of occupied sites for any period in our study (Voorhies 1989b:123). Also noteworthy is the

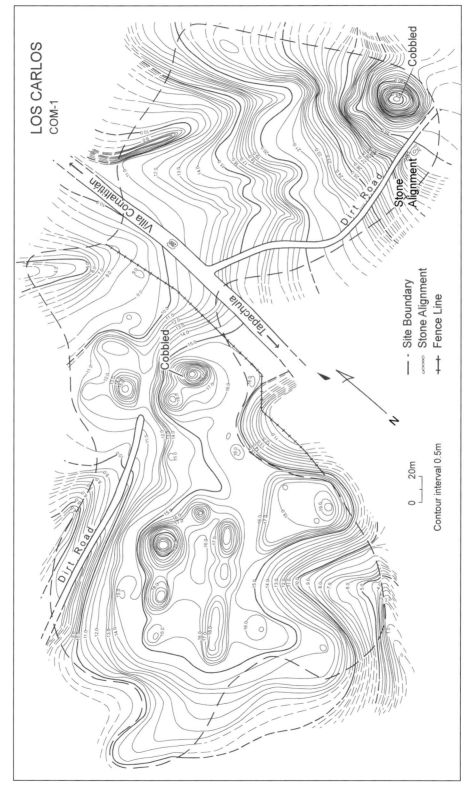

Figure 3.18. Topographic map of Los Carlos (mapped by J. Gasco, D. Hosler, and L. Pfeiffer; drafted by A. Nethery).

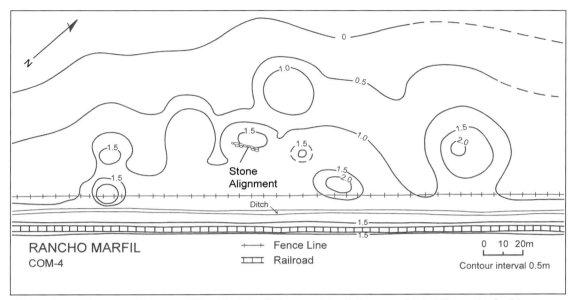

Figure 3.19 Topographic map of Rancho Marfil (mapped by S. Levy and J. Mallory; drafted by A. Nethery).

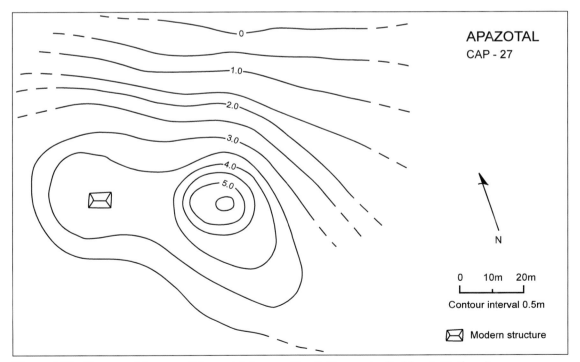

Figure 3.20. Topographic map of Apazotal (mapped by J. Gasco; drafted by A. Nethery).

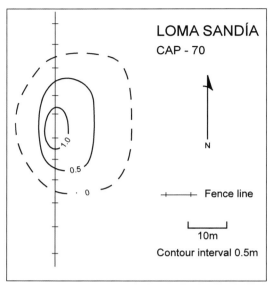

Figure 3.21. Topographic map of Loma Sandía (mapped with compass, tape, and level by A. Gerstle, S. Levy, and J. Mallory; drafted by A. Nethery)

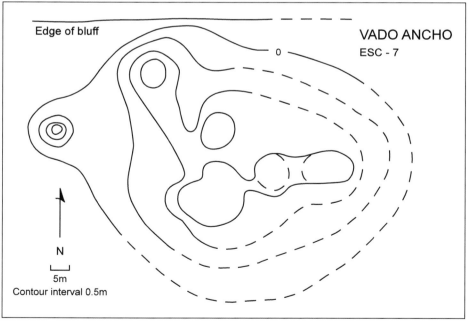

Figure 3.22. Topographic map of Vado Ancho (sketch map by M. Jaffe; drafted by A. Nethery).

fact that the Early Classic sites are distributed rather uniformly across the study area (Figure 3.1) and occur in all of its major environmental zones. Using the number of sites as a very crude and imperfect measure of population size, the data suggest a steady demographic increase from the Late Archaic period to the Early Classic period (see discussion in Voorhies [1989b]). Or, if the regional population did not actually increase numerically, the site data are unambiguous that the inhabitants of the study area first expanded into all environmental zones at this time.

We also noted previously that most sites occupied during the Early Classic period continued to be occupied during the Late Classic period, rendering it very difficult to identify intrasite settlement layouts for the Early Classic period. Moreover, most of the sites considered in the present chapter are small and consist of only one to six small, low mounds. We suspect that these sites are the archaeological signatures of isolated rural households. That is, we suggest that the mounds once supported houses or other domestic structures, although this has not been verified by subsurface investigations. These possible small and exclusively residential sites are: Amatillo (CAP-28), Lomas San Francisco (CAP-48), Lomas San Juan (CAP-49), Rancho Ancheta (ESC-4), Lomas Flor (ESC-5), Loma José (ESC-6), Apazotal (CAP-27), Loma Sandía (CAP-70), and Vado Ancho (ESC-7). An additional site, Rancho Marfil (COM-4) may also belong with this group of sites. It has eight surviving mounds and has been partially destroyed by railroad construction, so its original appearance is difficult to determine.

Four additional sites, Tepalcatenco (CAC-1), Panteón (ESC-1) Zorrillo (CAP-62), and Los Carlos (COM-1), have more platform mounds, and these are larger compared with the mounds in the residential group. Thus, these settlements must have had larger populations compared with the rural households and may have had a wider range of sociopolitical functions (but see Chapter 6). Another characteristic that sets these sites apart from the presumed residential sites is that they have at least one tall, conical platform mound around which are scattered the small,

low mounds that have broad upper surfaces. The tall, conical mounds are likely to have had a social function other than a residential one, and we surmise, based on the general Mesoamerican pattern, that their purpose was ritual.

Nonetheless, in the first three sites mentioned there is no formal site layout and no delineated plazas apparent to us in the site plans. Rather, the only discernible pattern is that at Panteón and Tepalcatenco each conical mound has a cluster of smaller mounds surrounding it, and together these form a spatial group that is separate from other such groups. Accordingly, we hypothesize that each of these architectural groups is a signature of a distinct social group, perhaps a kin-based group such as a lineage or a clan. There are two prominent conical mounds at Zorrillo, but they are close together, and the low mounds around them do not form spatially separate clusters.

The Los Carlos site does not seem to conform at all to the pattern we have described. This site has a high mound that is perched on a hilltop, but a few small low mounds are found in its vicinity. Moreover, the site has a formal, rectangular plaza that is formed by seven mounds, delimiting three of the plaza's sides. It is possible that this plaza was constructed during the Late Classic period, since we know that the site was occupied at that time. We do not have the data necessary to determine whether formal site layouts were adopted in the study area prior to the Late Classic period, but this site would be an excellent place to investigate this issue.

Finally, we note that no ballcourts are present in the sites discussed in this chapter. This absence is striking in view of the fact that ballcourts are common at the contemporary site of Los Horcones at the northwest end of the Chiapas coast (García-Des Lauriers 2007), and in sites within our study area that were abandoned in the Late Classic period (Chapter 4). From these limited data we deduce that formal ball courts were not being constructed in the study area during the Early Classic period; however, this inference is based upon a small sample and may be found to be incorrect.

In Chapter 6 we return to the issue of site hierarchies and what further inferences might be possible about regional sociopolitical organization based upon these limited data for the Early Classic period.

A final set of observations concern a very small inventory of burials. The preservation of bone is very poor in the study area, with the exception of sites located where the water table is high. Despite these conditions, Linda Pfeiffer recovered three burials from Río Arriba that date to the Early Classic period, and Hector Neff recovered a Protoclassic burial from Las Morenas. The details of these four burials, along with other burials from the study area, appear in Appendix A: Human Burials.

All four burials were in simple pits and were located in areas adjacent to the platform mounds rather than within the fill of platform mounds. One mature male at Río Arriba may have been adorned with a shell necklace when he was buried, but no other grave goods were associated with the four burials. The above-mentioned male may have suffered a blow to the head, and his left leg bones were missing. The evidence of cranial trauma might indicate the presence of societal violence, but a simple accident certainly cannot be ruled out. The significance of missing leg bones is also open to conjecture: we do not know if the leg was amputated during life or if the bones were curated as reliquaries.

In summary, our data are so limited for this time period that firm conclusions cannot be made. Still, we have proposed some ideas for future investigation.

CHAPTER 4

SITES WITH FINAL, LATE CLASSIC PERIOD OCCUPATIONS

We identified 66 sites in the site inventory as having been occupied during the Late Classic period (Figure 1.5), which is the third largest number of sites for any time period in our analysis (Voorhies 1989b). The locations of the known Late Classic period sites are shown on Figure 4.1. The sites are not only numerous, but they are distributed rather evenly over the entire study area from the foothills to the wetlands. In other words, it appears from our regional settlement data that the population living in the study area during the Late Classic period was fairly substantial and also widely dispersed like that of the Early Classic period.

Unlike the situation for the Early Classic period, many of the Late Classic period settlements were abandoned or nearly abandoned at the end of that period. As may be seen in Figure 1.5, there are 35 sites with primary occupations in the Late Classic period that were never reoccupied, according to our available evidence. This represents 53 percent of the total number of sites known to have been in use during the same time period. Moreover, many of the Late Classic period sites that were occupied in the Late Postclassic period apparently were used by only small groups of people, such as extended families. Such sites (N=12) are shown as having either secondary or tertiary levels of occupation in the histogram. This means that 71 percent of sites in our inventory that were occupied during the Late Classic period were either unoccupied, or occupied in a minor way after the end of that period. This observation must mean that a major societal change occurred at the end of the Late Classic period. This could either have been a major demographic collapse (due to high mortality or out-migration) resulting in a reduced population in the area, or, alternatively, the population may have substantially reorganized itself into fewer but larger settlements.

This finding contrasts sharply with the situation at the end of the Early Classic period as we discussed in the last chapter. It is possible that because of our failure to recognize the Early Postclassic period artifacts the apparent site abandonment did not actually take place, at least in the synchronized way that is indicated by our data. We find ourselves in exactly the same position as Mayanists some time ago when site abandonment of the southern Maya lowlands was apparent, but there was no agreement as to whether this was due to a major decline in the regional population or simply an abandonment of higher order centers as a result of a change in the social organization of the community.

Although our data are far from conclusive, all evidence available points to a major social and demographic change in the western Soconusco at the end of the Late Classic period; currently, the nature of this change is not understood.

SITE DESCRIPTIONS

We now describe 47 sites with substantial, final Late Classic period occupations. The first three sites shown on the histogram (Figure 1.5) with final occupations in the Late Classic period are included in Appendix B: Miscellaneous Sites because they have various unique features. These are Palillo (CAP-19), Mataxte (CAP-20), and San Andrés (CAP-25).

Campíto (CAP-15)

Campíto is situated on a long island formed by an inactive barrier beach, southwest of Laguna Campón. At this site there are 21 platform mounds within an area measuring approximately 4.06 ha (Figure 4.2). The largest mounds at the site enclose a rectangular open plaza, and this zone is the apparent public center of the site. The highest mound at the site, at

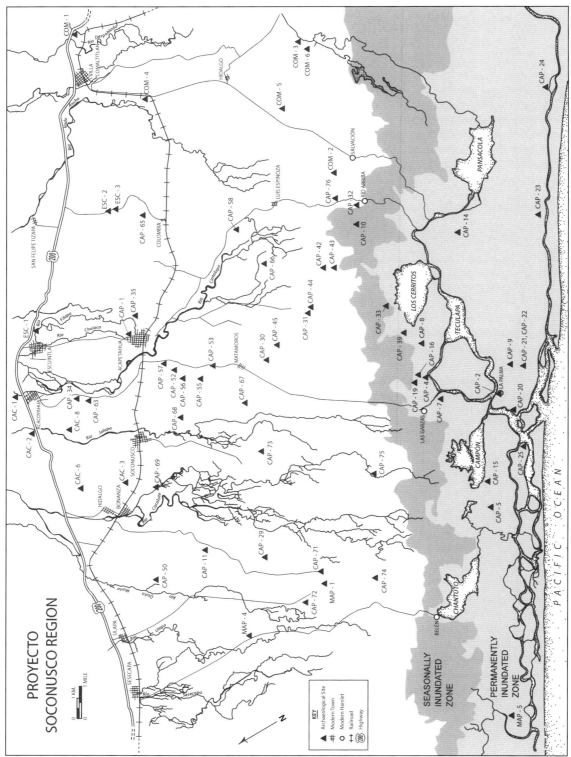

Figure 4.1. Archaeological sites occupied during the Late Classic period (from Voorhies 1989b:Fig. 5.14).

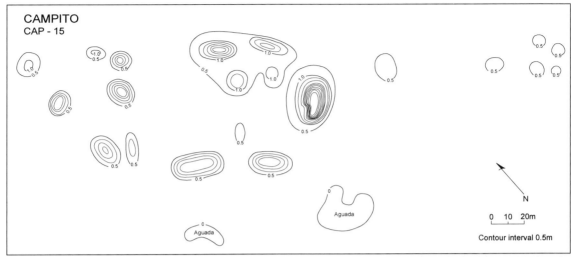

Figure 4.2. Topographic map of Campíto (mapped by J. Gasco and B. Voorhies; drafted by A. Nethery).

5 m, delimits the eastern side of the plaza. At the eastern edge of the open area there are two proximate and parallel mounds that are possibly a ball court. Two ponds are south of the plaza. It is likely that the cluster of small, very low mounds at the eastern part of the site center represents residential platforms.

The site is relatively undisturbed, although we observed a few looters' excavations. Surface material was scarce because surface disturbance at the site was minimal. Our analysis of the collected ceramics suggests to us that the major occupation occurred during the Early-Late Classic period. Lighter occupations occurred during the Early-Middle Preclassic and in the Late Postclassic. The attribution of an Early Postclassic occupation is based solely on a single Tohil Plumbate effigy vessel that the site owner, Rafael Ovalle Hilerio, donated to the regional museum of anthropology and history in Tuxtla Gutiérrez.

La Cancha (CAP-50)

This site is located in the northwest quadrant of the study area on the flat coastal plain south of the railroad station Ulapa. It lies east of the Río Doña María and was discovered during the survey of Transect B-8 (Figure 1.9).

The site consists of five mounds, two of which form a ball court, the most prominent feature of the site (Figure 4.3). These two

mounds are long, narrow, and oblong in shape and are only 4 m apart. The three other mounds at the site are less than 0.5 m high, whereas the platform mounds of the ball court are 1 m high. The site area is 1.15 ha. This is the only site in our sample where a ball court is disassociated from other apparent public structures. Although this may be because other mounds at the site were destroyed, we have no evidence that this was the case.

Our analysis of the surface ceramics dates the site to the Late Preclassic through Late Classic periods.

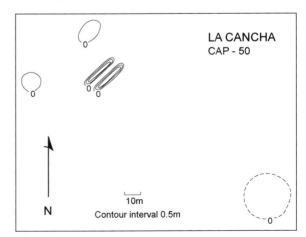

Figure 4.3. Planimetric map of La Cancha (surveyed with pace and compass by S. Levy and J. Mallory; drafted by A. Nethery).

Lomas Gutiérrez (CAP-69)

Lomas Gutiérrez is located on the flat coastal plain, approximately 1.5 km south of Bonanza. It is on the eastern bank of a stream channel that is part of the Río Cacaluta drainage system. The site was discovered during the survey of Transect F-12 (Figure 1.19).

This is a small site measuring only 0.58 ha and consisting of two oblong mounds, the highest of which is 3.5 m (Figure 4.4).

According to our analysis of surface collected ceramics the site was occupied from the Late Preclassic-Late Classic periods. From its appearance we conjecture that the site was a residential location.

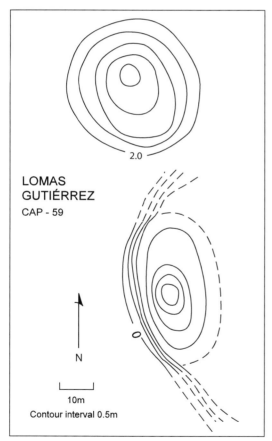

Figure 4.4. Topographic map of Lomas Gutiérrez (sketch map by S. Levy and J. Mallory; drafted by A. Nethery)

Nicolás Bravo (MAP-4)

Nicolás Bravo is located on the flat coastal plain, east of the Río Ulapa. There is a central high, conical mound that is surrounded by other mounds that do not exhibit a highly formal pattern (Figure 4.5). The principal mound stands 3.5 m high and possibly forms the eastern boundary of a plaza group. Other large mounds in this vicinity might have had public rather than residential functions. Low mounds are located toward the periphery of the site, and we suspect that they are residential in function. MAP-4 has a ball court located at the western edge of the site. It is obvious that some of the platform mounds have retaining walls constructed of waterworn cobbles as these may be seen eroding from them.

We mapped 38 mounds in an area measuring 15.05 ha. According to our analysis of surface ceramics, the site was occupied from the Late Preclassic through Late Classic periods.

Las Campanitas (CAC-6)

Las Campanitas is located in the lowest foothills of the coastal range to the east of Ejido Hidalgo between the Pan American Highway and the rail line. The site sprawls over an area of approximately 19.58 ha, within which we mapped 19 mounds (Figure 4.6). As is usual for many of the Classic period sites of the study area, one mound is higher than the others and it is centrally located. In this case the tallest mound is 3 m above the adjacent ground level. Three other mounds, presumably with public functions, are in a line immediately to the west of the tall mound. Other low mounds are scattered widely over the mapped area of the site.

A highly unusual characteristic of this site is the cluster of approximately 17 stone-faced graves located northwest of the tall mound. These probably date to sometime after the Spanish Conquest because this grave type is typically European and not a Mesoamerican burial pattern. Each of the graves consisted of a hummock of earth with protective stones laid upon it. The construction of the graves was simple; no mortar or cut stone was used. There were no grave markers or other clues to the

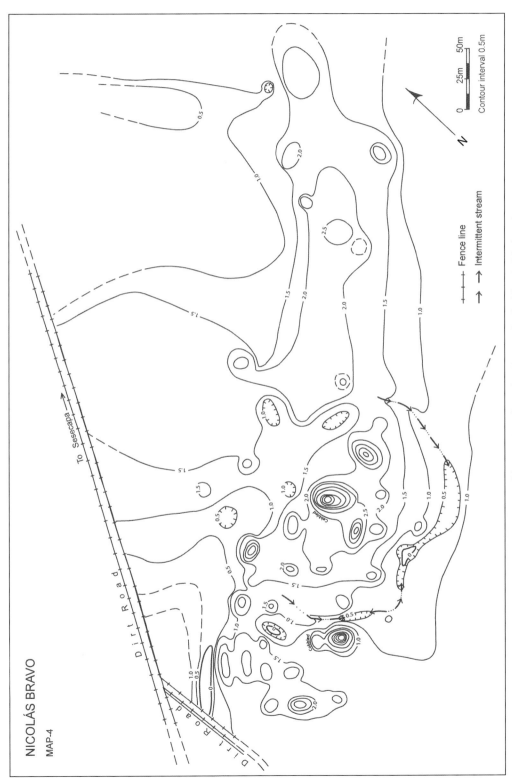

Figure 4.5. Topographic map of Nicolás Bravo (mapped by A. Gerstle and S. Levy; drafted by A. Nethery).

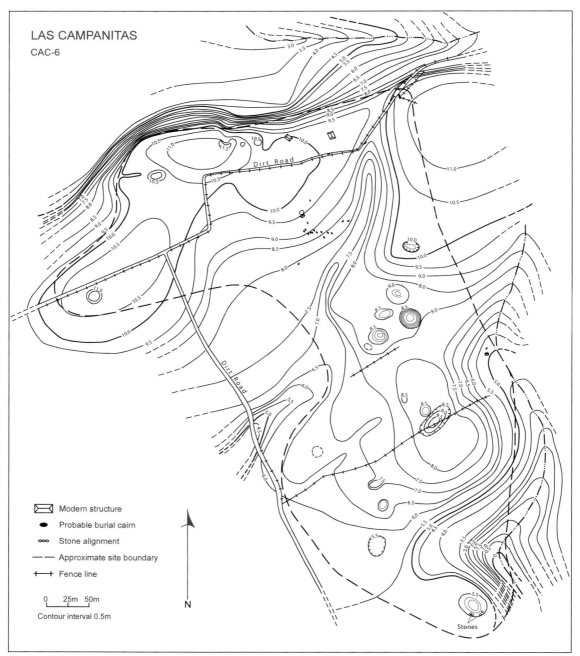

Figure 4.6. Topographic map of Las Campanitas (mapped by J. Gasco, L. Pfeiffer and D. Hosler; drafted by A. Nethery).

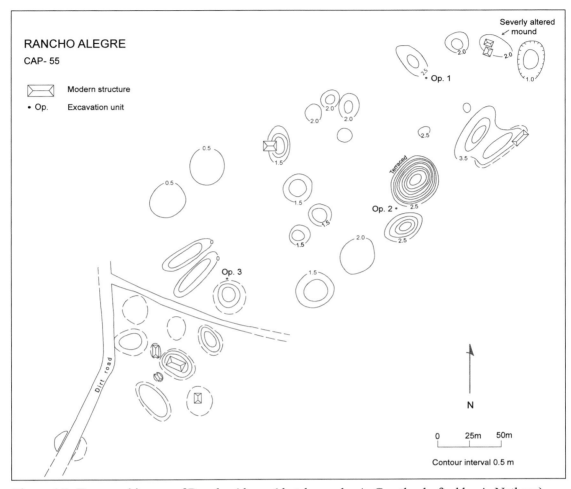

Figure 4.7. Topographic map of Rancho Alegre (sketch map by A. Gerstle; drafted by A. Nethery).

antiquity of the graves, but we suspect that this cemetery dates to the historic period.

The Prehispanic occupation of the site spanned the Late Preclassic through the Late Classic, according to our analysis of ceramics collected from the site surface.

Rancho Alegre (CAP-55)

Rancho Alegre is located west of the road from Acapetahua to Matamoros and is a little over one km north of that town. The site is situated on flat terrain. The site area is 7.28 ha, within which we have mapped 34 mounds (Figure 4.7). One mound is steep sided and taller (> 4.0 m) than the others. Other lower platform mounds in the near vicinity of the tall mound are

arranged to form what appear to be two semi-formal plazas. The site has two ball courts, one on either side of the principal mound. Cobbles are present on the slopes of the tallest mound and many others, indicating that some platform mounds were cobble faced.

At the time of our study much of the site was a cacao orchard, which made mapping difficult because of reduced visibility. It is entirely possible that we missed some of the lowest mounds at the site.

On the basis of analysis of surface and subsurface ceramics we date the site from the beginning of the Late Preclassic through the Late Classic, with the most intense occupation in the Late Classic period. We excavated three test pits, the locations of which are plotted on Figure 4.7. The results of these excavations are discussed below.

Operation 1. A 1 by 2 m test pit was excavated in the northeast section of the site by field assistant Clare Yarborough. The test pit was placed near the base of a low platform mound. A thin layer of volcanic ash was encountered at a depth of 0.14 to 0.21 m below the surface over much of the tested area, but in one spot historic glass and other indicators of disturbance extended to approximately a half meter in depth. No construction features were noted until a possible cobble pavement was uncovered at approximately 0.77 m below the ground surface. With the exception of a miniature mask (FN #4919), very few artifacts were recovered above the cobble feature, but several pieces of obsidian and possible mano fragments were mixed in with the cobbles comprising the base of the pavement. However, the highest frequency of sherds found in the test pit occurred directly underneath the cobble feature, at a depth of 0.91 to 1.01 m below the surface. No sherds were found below a depth of 1.11 m. Excavation continued through sterile soils to 1.36 m below the surface and was followed by an auger probe to 1.90 m which exposed alluvial clay.

Operation 2. Field assistant John Carpenter excavated a 1 by 1 m test pit at the base of the largest mound at Rancho Alegre. No features were encountered in this unit. The highest density of artifacts was recovered between depths of 0.50 to 0.90 m below the ground surface. These artifacts included numerous ceramic sherds, three ceramic ear spools (FN #4935, #4936, and #4937), an obsidian core, and several blade fragments. Approximately 40 of the 50 obsidian pieces from this unit were located within the layer of high artifact density. Several cobbles were found between 0.70 and 0.80 m. Soil 1, a silty clay, began below the upper disturbed zone (0.30 m), and continued to a depth of one meter below the surface. So few artifacts were found within the Soil 2 matrix (a fine-grained sandy clay) that excavations ceased with the beginning of Soil 3 at depth of 1.20 m. An auger test probed to 1.70 m below the

surface, passing through a fourth soil type and retrieving no artifacts.

Operation 3. Field assistant Ann Bennett excavated a 1 by 1 m test pit near a mound southeast of the ball court. A thin lens of ash was encountered at approximately 0.15 m below the ground surface. A layer of cobbles was found in the unit between 0.70 m to 0.80 m below the surface. Here the cobbles were not as densely packed as those in Operation 1. More artifacts, including both sherds and obsidian fragments, were found directly above and below the cobbles compared with the rest of the unit. Beginning at 0.90 m, a feature hypothesized to be a trash pit began to be exposed in the southeast corner of the unit. It was marked by a clayey rather than sandy soil matrix, and contained numerous flat-lying sherds at its top and abundant artifacts throughout. The soil surrounding this feature was removed to a depth of 1.20 m, and was found to be sterile. The pit feature terminated at 1.30 m below the surface. An auger was used to probe to a depth of 1.90 m, encountering a sandy soil containing waterworn pebbles.

The site owner has a small collection of artifacts that were found on his property. Among these is a ceramic hand holding an oblong object that we first thought was a cacao pod (Figure 4.8). John Clark, who examined this artifact, doubts this interpretation. The object looks like it should be a fruit, but we have been unable to determine what it is. This item is made of low-fired, coarse-tempered, unslipped ware and must be from a large statue or effigy incense burner such as those reported by Drucker (1948).

Los Descansados (CAP-66)

Los Descansados is approximately 3.8 km northwest of the town of Luis Espinoza. It was discovered by an exhausted field crew (hence its name), who had strayed beyond the terminus of the first transect that was walked. The site is small, measuring only 2.04 ha, within which we have mapped nine mounds (Figure 4.9). The tallest mound at the site is only a meter high, and it is not significantly taller than the other mounds associated with it. These mounds enclose an area that is roughly circular in shape.

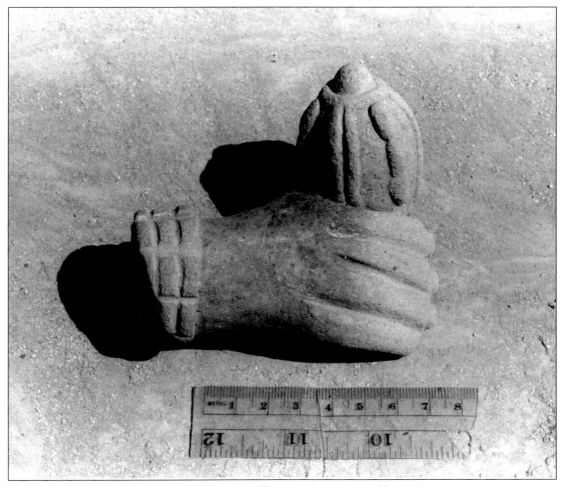

Figure 4.8. Photograph of hand from a large effigy holding oblong object.

What is surprising to us is the presence of a ball court at this small and otherwise apparently unimportant site.

Surface sherds indicate that the site was occupied from the beginning of the Late Preclassic through the Late Classic, with the most intense occupation during the Middle-Late Classic period.

Las Lomas (COM-6)

Las Lomas is located near the western edge of the study area, south of Villa Comaltitlán and on the lower gradient of the coastal plain. It is situated on flat terrain, near a seasonal stream. The site area is 15.38 ha, within which are 114

platform mounds (Figure 4.10). Las Lomas has the second largest number of platform mounds in the site inventory. Acapetahua, the site with the greatest number of mounds, actually consists of two distinct zones occupied during different periods, whereas it is possible that at Las Lomas all mounds were in use simultaneously. Furthermore, the mound density at Las Lomas is exceptionally high. In other words, the site plan of Las Lomas suggests that this was once a relatively large community compared with other settlements within the study area.

The site was arranged so that the larger, presumably public-oriented platform mounds are toward the center of the site and lower,

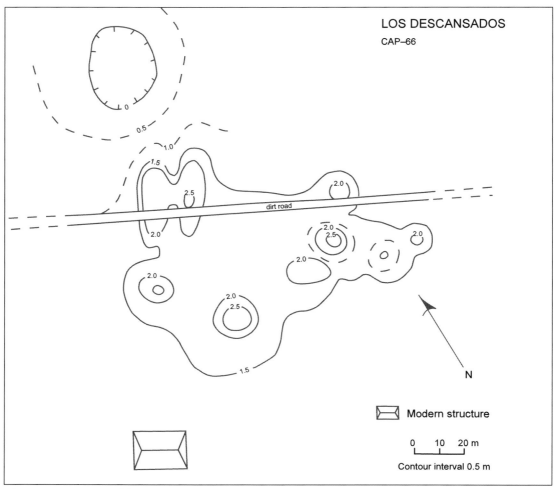

Figure 4.9. Topographic map of Los Descansados (sketch map by S. Levy and J. Mallory; drafted by A. Nethery).

presumably residential mounds are toward the site periphery. The tallest mound, possibly a temple platform, is 3.5 m high. It forms part of a row of mounds. We detect four such parallel mound rows that delineate three open corridors or long narrow plazas. The linear arrangement of these mounds is similar to that in the Classic Period center at Acapetahua (discussed below). A ball court is at the eastern edge of the site near the stream channel. There is also a large depression that may be a stone-lined reservoir as at Acapetahua; however, this possibility was not tested.

According to our analysis of both surface and subsurface ceramics, the site was occupied from the beginning of the Late Preclassic through the Late Classic periods. The most intense occupation appears to have been during the Middle-Late Classic. Some Late Postclassic material suggests that there was a light occupation during that time. Four test pits were excavated at the site, and these are discussed below.

Operation 1. Field assistant Clare Yarborough excavated a 1.5 by 1.5 m test pit in the northeast portion of the site. The excavation

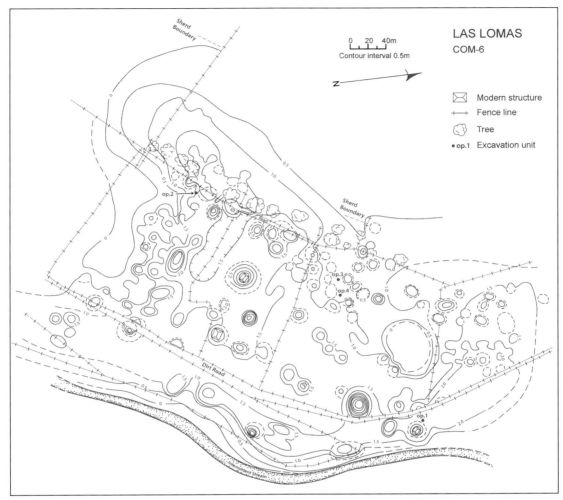

Figure 4.10. Topographic map of Las Lomas (mapped by A. Gerstle, M. Jaffe, S. Levy, and J. Mallory; drafted by A. Nethery).

was placed on a level surface between two platform mounds and near the present day stream channel. The upper strata, including soils 1 and 2, as well as the dark charcoal-bearing stratum, contain both modern and prehistoric material and are clearly disturbed (Figure 4.11), most likely caused by modern farming activities. The volcanic ash characteristic of the region was noted in isolated patches between 0.16 and 0.26 m below the surface, probably from the 1902 eruption of the Santa María Volcano. Construction fill was found at approximately 0.77 m; it was characterized by dark clay mixed

with pieces of daub. Nonetheless, we could not determine the original form of this feature. The first midden deposit (Midden 1), ranging 0.20 to 0.40 m in thickness and labeled Soil 6, was encountered at 0.95 m below the surface. Items of note recovered from this midden, in addition to numerous sherds, bone, ground stone, and obsidian, include a pair of ear ornaments (FN #83-4854, #83-4860), two figurine fragments (FN #83-4856), and two greenstone celts (FN #83-4855, #83-4859). Directly below Midden 1 in some areas lay an olive brown clay lens (Soil 9). A second midden (Midden 2), labeled Soil

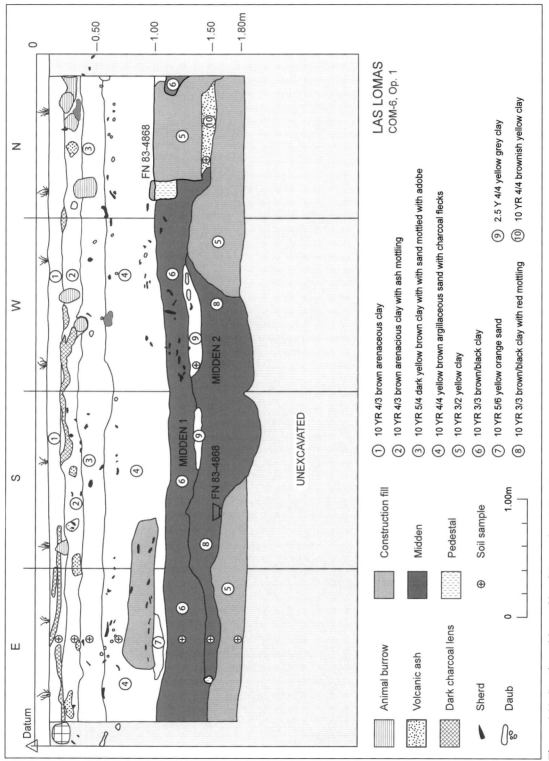

Figure 4.11. Stratigraphic profile of Operation 1, Las Lomas.

8, began at a depth of 1.20 m below the ground surface, and extended down to 1.70 m in some sections of the unit. Artifacts found within the midden include a complete vessel (FN #83-4868), a ceramic ocarina (FN #83-4866), a small clay ball (FN #83-4863), a hammerstone (FN #83-4870), and a turtle carapace (FN #83-4867). Evidence for burning was noted near the base of this midden: burned sherds, burned bone, burned adobe, and numerous pieces of charcoal were recovered. Sterile soil (Soil 5) was encountered under some areas of Midden 2.

Although this small test pit gives only a glimpse of subsurface contents and structure of the archaeological deposits, it seems likely that we have penetrated domestic trash, which supports the idea that the nearby mounds were residential in function.

Operation 2. Field assistant John Carpenter excavated a 1.5 by 1.5 m test pit in the southwest quadrant of Las Lomas, near the limit of the site. The excavation was placed on a level area among a cluster of low platform mounds. Carpenter removed the topsoil (Soil 1), which had modern disturbance (Figure 4.12). The underlying soil (Soil 2) contained sherds, chipped stone items, and adobe fragments. A few pockets of volcanic ash, again presumably from the 1902 volcanic eruption, were noted at approximately 0.12 to 0.15 m below the surface. Abundant cultural material was recovered from a dark colored and malodorous clay layer (Soil 3) extending from 0.30 to 0.80 m below the datum. These artifacts included ceramic sherds, bone fragments, many pieces of adobe or burned clay, a chip of turquoise (FN #83-4943), and chipped stone objects of obsidian and chert. A hard-packed prepared floor (Soil 4) 2 to 4 cm thick was encountered at 0.80 m. A dark midden (Soil 5) was found directly underneath this occupational surface; the midden extended from 0.84 to 0.98 m and showed evidence of being burnt. The artifacts from this midden layer consisted mainly of sherds, but obsidian and chert artifacts, bone, and a ceramic ocarina (FN #83-4948) were also found. Beneath Midden 1 was a layer of clay (Soil 6) with only a few artifacts. This was underlain by Midden 2 (Soil 7), which was encountered at 1.12 m below

the ground surface. Midden 2, approximately 0.13 m thick, also exhibited signs of having been burned. It contained a high percentage of charcoal and burned clay, along with some burnt sherds. Soil 8, the underlying stratum, is a sandy clay layer containing relatively few artifacts, but a partially reconstructable vessel was recovered. Sterile soil (Soil 9) began at 1.65 m.

A human burial was found extending from 1.55 to 1.95 m below the surface along the south wall of the excavation unit. The burial pit, barely big enough to accommodate the osteological remains, was filled with a dark sandy clay (Soil 10). The articulated skeleton was seated facing west, with the hands placed on its feet. The individual's sex was not determined. Carpenter estimated that this individual was probably a young adult, based on moderate tooth wear and the presence of the upper wisdom teeth. In addition, all the observable epiphyses and sutures were fused. Carpenter also noted that the one observable humerus measured 30 cm and may be indicative of the individual having been of tall stature. The incisors were shovel shaped, and a supernumerary tooth was seen behind the upper incisors. No grave goods were found with the burial. The osteological materials were not removed, and the unit was backfilled with the burial in situ. We left the burial in place at the request of the landowner.

Our overall conclusions are that we encountered two domestic midden deposits, which suggests to us that the platform mounds in the immediate vicinity are residential.

Operation 3. Field assistant Ann Bennett excavated a 1.5 by 1.5 m test pit in a level area north of the site's principal mound. Low platform mounds surround the excavation location. The topsoil (Soil 1) contained only a few artifacts and is less than ten centimeters thick (Figure 4.13). The underlying Soil 2 has a noticeably higher sherd density. Pockets of volcanic ash were encountered from 0.10 to 0.20 m below the surface and we think that the ash originated from the 1902 Santa Maria eruption. In the upper 0.20 m Bennett found modern materials mixed with prehistoric artifacts. Similar to Operation 2, a dark silty clay (Soil 3) that "smelled like swamp soil"

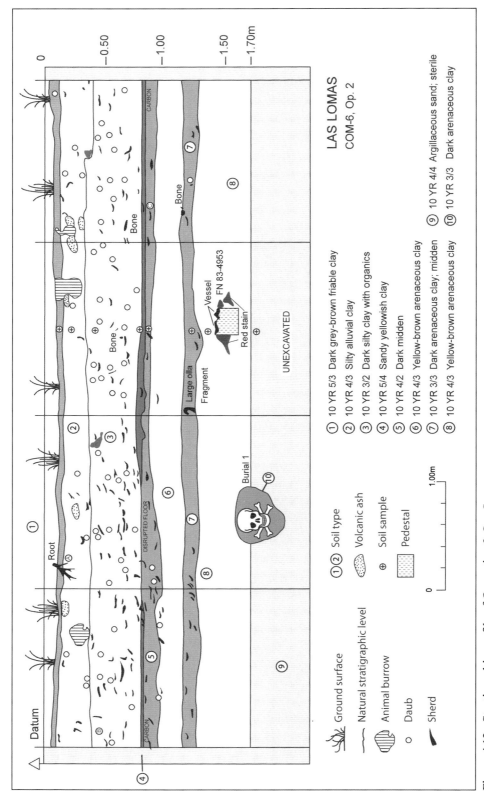

Figure 4.12. Stratigraphic profile of Operation 2, Las Lomas.

extended from 0.20 to 0.43 m. Many daub fragments were recovered from this level, along with numerous large sherds, as well as chert and obsidian fragments. A hearth was found within the 0.40-0.50 m level within Soil 3 and along the south side of the unit. The hearth was identified from several large stones and a roughly circular burned area that continued for almost 0.20 m below the rocks. Two hammerstones (FN 83-5036), a thermally cracked chert biface (FN 83-5037), and other miscellaneous chert artifacts were also associated with this feature. Numerous sherds, bone, daub, and artifacts of chert and obsidian continued to be found to a depth of 0.70 m. Below the 0.70 m level Bennett encountered Soil 6, which is devoid of artifacts except for those associated with two intrusive burials. A new soil (Soil 8) was encountered at the 1.60 m level in an auger probe.

The first burial (Burial 1) encountered was exposed along the east profile, beginning at a depth of 0.70 m. The skeleton was sitting tightly flexed within the burial pit. No grave goods were found, other than a few sherds that may have been associated with the burial. Bennett noticed that none of the observable bones had developed epiphyses. No toes were present on one foot, and Bennett thought that this may be an old injury. A large piece of ochre was found on top of the foot. The second burial was found at a depth of 1.23 m, also within Soil 6. Apparently an infant, the skeleton was disarticulated. Several sherds, a large piece of red ochre, and a gar pike scale were found associated with the osteological remains. Both of these burials were in a poor state of preservation. They were not removed from the unit in deference to the wishes of the landowner.

Operation 4. This 1.5 by 1.5 m test pit is located north of the central mound on a flat lying area near Operation 3. It was excavated by field assistant James M. Kules. The topsoil (Soil 1) is about 10 cm thick and is underlain by grayish tan clay with small pockets of volcanic ash (Figure 4.14). This soil is between 0.10 and 0.16 m in depth below the datum. A possible occupational surface (Soil 4) was found at 0.40 m and was distinguished by a 4-8 cm thick layer of compact clay. A midden (Midden 1) was

found directly underneath this surface. The soil within the midden (Soil 5) was a dark brown clay with a high content of organic matter and extended from 0.42 m to as much as 0.80 m in some places. Kules recovered quantities of obsidian from the midden, along with over 41 kg of ceramic sherds. In addition, burnt daub and charcoal-laden soil also were found, indicating that burning episodes had taken place. Several possible postholes were noted at a depth of 0.70 m; these circular features extended to 0.90 m. A second midden (Midden 2) directly underlies Midden 1. It, too, contained abundant charcoal and artifacts. Soil 6 may be construction fill. It is a yellow-brown arenaceous clay containing much less cultural material compared with the overlying middens and becomes sterile at approximately 1.20 m. Excavations ceased at a depth of 1.40 m, but an auger hole was bored to 2.42 m and no additional cultural material was found. A soil change was noted at 1.70 m.

The Las Lomas site is intriguing because of the high density and number of platform mounds at the site and its exceptionally good preservation. It is the only site inland of the wetlands in the study area for which we have bone preservation. This is due, it seems, to the anaerobic soil conditions noted by the excavators.

Dos Amates (CAC-2)

The site of Dos Amates is located in the foothills of the coastal range. The site is readily visible from the Pan American Highway and from the access road to Colonia Soconusco, both of which traverse the site (Figure 4.15). We found the site through casual observation.

The site is 5.53 ha, and within this area we mapped 25 mounds. The main focus of the site plan is on the northern side of the highway, where the site's highest mound (5.0 m) forms part of a formal plaza group. On the south side of the highway the mounds are less dense, and artifacts were less frequent compared with the northern plaza area.

Some mounds clearly had retaining walls constructed of cobbles. The owner of the site reported that formerly there were many stone sculptures representing jaguars; however, we did

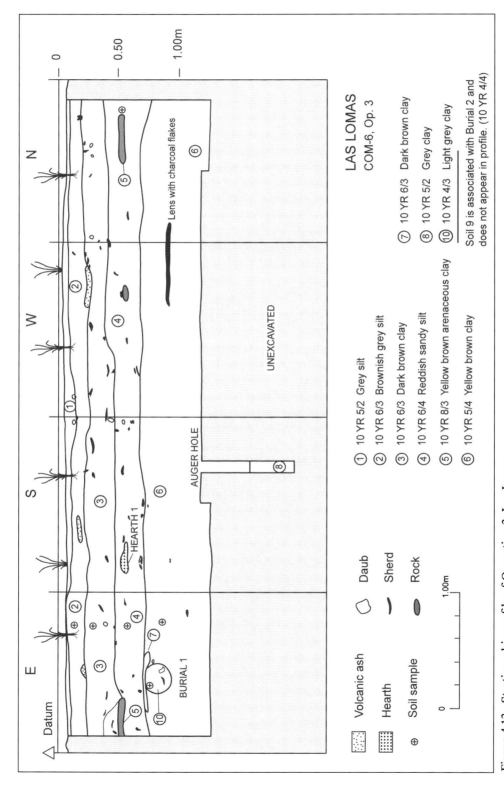

Figure 4.13. Stratigraphic profile of Operation 3, Las Lomas.

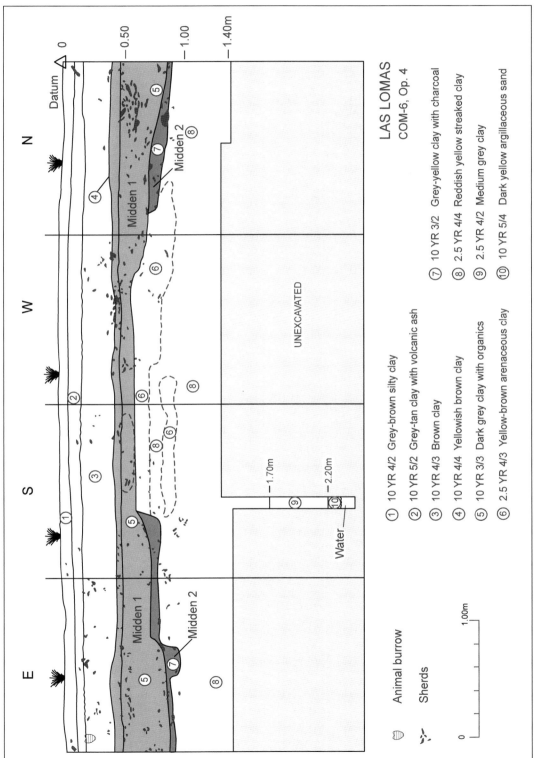

Figure 4.14. Stratigraphic profile of Operation 4, Las Lomas.

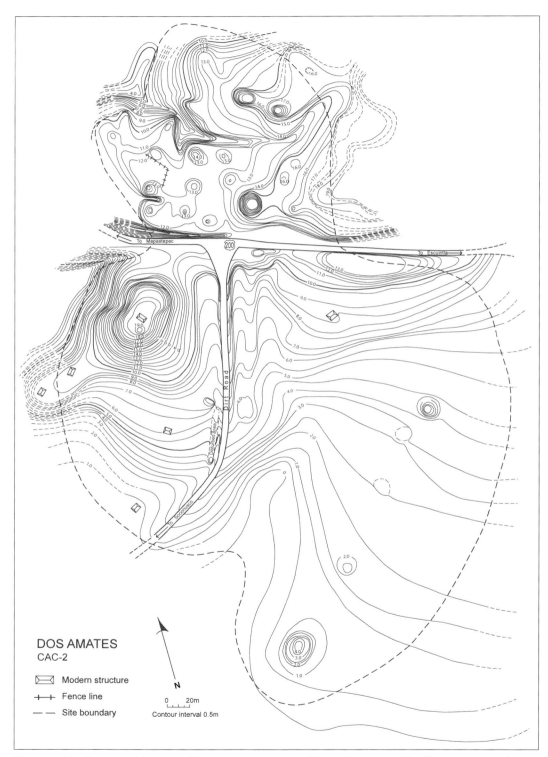

Figure 4.15. Topographic map of Dos Amates (mapped by J. Gasco, L. Pfeiffer, and D. Hosler; drafted by A. Nethery).

not observe any pieces of stone sculpture on the site surface, and we did not learn what happened to the reported sculptures.

The site was occupied from the Late Preclassic through the Late Classic periods, with a less intense occupation during the Late Postclassic period.

La Concepción (CAP-24)

La Concepción is located at the southeast margin of the study area, south of Laguna Pansacola. The site is situated within the mangrove formation on an island formed by an inactive barrier beach. It is strategically located at the edge of the inland waterway thought by us to have been important in ancient times as a transportation route.

The earliest mention of La Concepción in an archaeological context known to us is Drucker's (1948:159) report of a small effigy plumbate vessel said to have come from the site and noted by him as being in a private collection. Drucker did not visit the site, and its location, marked on his map (Drucker 1948:152) with a question mark, is placed incorrectly. Navarrete's map (NWAF map archives) accurately locates the site, but since it is marked with a question mark, it is probable that Navarrete did not visit it.

The area covered by the map encompasses 5.28 ha (Figure 4.16). Twenty-two mounds have been mapped, the highest of which is 3.0 m above adjacent level ground. The basic site plan is that the tallest mound is centrally located, with other large and presumably public platform mounds forming an open rectangular plaza around it. Small low mounds, presumably habitation platforms, are farther from the public area. We are certain more of these low mounds are present, but at the time of mapping they were obscured by heavy vegetation.

According to our analysis of the surface ceramics, the major occupation of the site occurred from the Late Preclassic through the Late Classic periods. An Early Postclassic occupation is based on the Tohil Plumbate vessel reported by Drucker, and the Late Postclassic occupation is based on ceramics. Because of the presence of polychrome pottery dating from this last period, we have inferred the presence

of elites. For this rather dubious reason, the site was placed by Voorhies and Gasco (2004:60-61) in the second tier of the site hierarchy for the Late Postclassic period.

Herrado (CAP-5)

The site of Herrado is located within the wetlands, southeast of Laguna Chantuto. It is situated on an inactive beach bearing the same name as the site. Navarrete reported the site during his 1969 survey of the region, although he may not have visited it since it is misplaced on his map. Drucker's field notes (n.d.:68) indicate that a local informant described the site to him.

We mapped the site and made surface collections during the first field season of Proyecto Soconusco. The site map (Figure 4.17) suggests it was a small public center consisting of nine mounds within an area of approximately 3.75 ha. The highest mound at the site is 7.0 m. The other platform mounds surround the tallest one.

The site was occupied from the Late Preclassic through the Late Classic periods. A less intense occupation during the Late Postclassic is indicated by the presence of sherds of that age.

El Conchal (CAP-14)

El Conchal is located northwest of Laguna Pansacola on an island within the mangrove forest formation. The site was discovered and named by Navarrete (NWAF map archives).

The site extends over the entire island, which measures 2.95 ha. The highest of the fourteen mounds is 6.0 m, and it is located in the approximate center of the elongated island (Figure 4.18). Large elongated mounds occur on the western, southern, and eastern peripheries of the site, but the north side is unobstructed by platform mounds. Perhaps access to the island originally was from the north. Now, however, the island is entered from the east. Two platform mounds form a ball court at the northeast corner of the site. There are also some smaller mounds in the vicinity of the central conical mound. There is no evident formal open plaza.

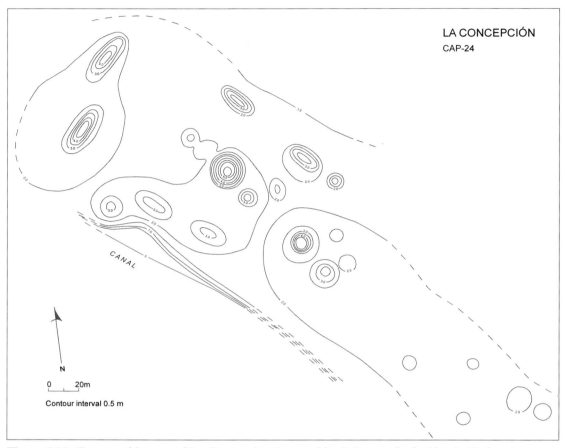

Figure 4.16. Topographic map of La Concepción (mapped by J. Gasco; drafted by A. Nethery); after Voorhies and Gasco (2004:Fig. 3.13).

Surface remains were relatively abundant and provided us with a comparatively large number of diagnostic sherds. On this basis we identify the main occupation from the Late Preclassic through Late Classic periods. A less intense occupation is indicated for the Late Postclassic Period. Surface remains included abundant marsh clam shells, as well as occasional shells of *Anadara* sp. A human bone fragment was found eroding out of a gully.

Subsequent to our earlier work John Hodgson cored the site and discovered layers predominately of shell that lie between 2 to 3 m below the surface. These were radiocarbon dated to the Late Archaic Period (Hodgson, personal communication). We have not included this information on our histogram (Figure 1-26)

since it was obtained after the study reported here.

Acapetahua (CAP-1)

Acapetahua is located on the eastern side of the town of the same name. This large site was occupied for an extended period of time, from at least the Late Preclassic through the Late Postclassic (and into modern times) with a possible hiatus during the Early Postclassic. This hiatus is likely to be more apparent than real due to difficulties in identifying the Early Postclassic period in our area (cf. Voorhies and Gasco 2004:11ff). Unlike the situation for most other sites in the Proyecto Soconusco study, we have sufficient subsurface evidence about Acapetahua to be able to distinguish a zone built during the

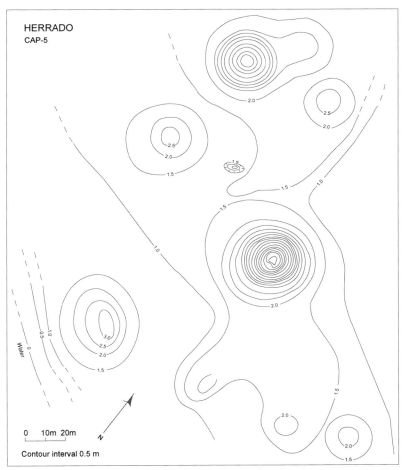

Figure 4.17. Topographic map of Herrado (mapped by J. Gasco and B. Voorhies; drafted by A. Nethery).

Classic period and another zone constructed mainly in the Postclassic. The entire site covers 42 ha.

We have previously published a description of the site and our work there (Voorhies and Gasco 2004:14), so only a brief description is warranted here. The Classic period platform mounds are located on the flat floodplain of the Río Chalaca (Figure 4.19), part of the Río Cintalapa system. We determined that the major occupation in this area was during the Classic period based on information from test pits placed in locations between mounds and from excavations in several mounds.

An open area, presumably a plaza, is bounded on the northern side by a row of

mounds, one of which (Mound 52) we excavated (Voorhies and Gasco 2004:32ff). It was constructed during the Middle to Late Classic time period. A second row of mounds parallels the first one along the side away from the plaza. The plaza is bounded on the east and west by other mounds and on the south in part by a ball court, which was constructed during the Late Classic period. The tallest mound (about 3.5 m) in this area is approximately at the center the public area and is among the mounds in the row along the northern edge of the plaza. At the eastern edge of this part of the site there is a pond. Auger tests demonstrated that it is a stone-lined reservoir. In general, the site plan of the Classic period center bears a strong resemblance

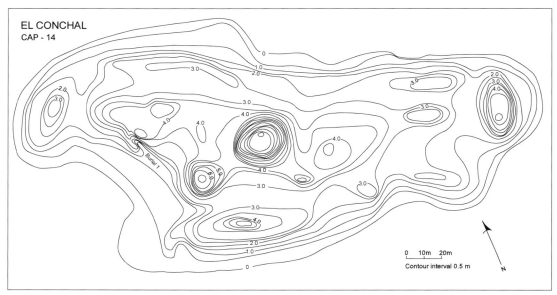

Figure 4.18. Topographic map of El Conchal (mapped by H. Neff, J. Gasco, and B. Voorhies; drafted by A. Nethery).

to the site of Las Lomas, which was occupied contemporaneously. Our excavations in this area have been described in detail elsewhere (Voorhies and Gasco 2004).

Altamirano (CAP-30)

Altamirano is located a short distance south of Matamoros in the middle section of the coastal plain. The site is situated on fairly level ground, but there is a stand of herbaceous swamp close to the site. This site was first discovered by Navarrete (NWAF map archives) and was rediscovered by us during the first field season of Proyecto Soconusco. Initially, Voorhies learned of its existence from a local informant, but subsequently the site was detected by the field crew walking Transect A-12 (Figure 1.6).

The site consists of three mound groups (Figure 4.20) that are separated by areas with no mounds. Nonetheless, the intervening areas have been plowed so it is possible that low mounds were once there and have now been leveled. The survey crew visited the site shortly after part of it had been plowed and because of this we recovered many artifacts from the site surface.

The site measures 27.32 ha in area, within which 33 platform mounds have been mapped. The distribution of these mounds is informal, except that the two highest mounds are in the approximate center of the site. These two high mounds are coalescing, with the higher of the two measuring 4.5 m above the adjacent level ground. Two mounds in the eastern mound cluster form a ball court.

The site was occupied from the Late Preclassic through the Late Classic periods.

Rancho Novillero (ESC-2)

Rancho Novillero straddles the road that runs from the Pan American Highway to the rail station at Colombia. The site is situated within the lowest foothills of the coastal range on hilly topography. The site covers an area of 13.58 ha, within which we have mapped 89 platform mounds (Figure 4.21). The tallest mound at the site is 2.5 m high. Northwest of this mound is an open plaza with a ball court forming the northern edge of this space. Most of the larger mounds at the site have cobbles eroding from their surfaces indicating that they are faced with rocks. This area is presumably the civic center

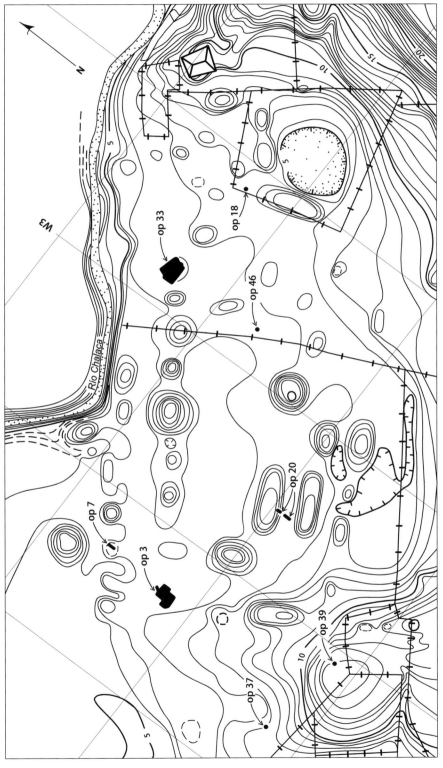

Figure 4.19. Partial topographic map of Acapetahua showing area built during the Classic period. Each grid is 100 m on a side.

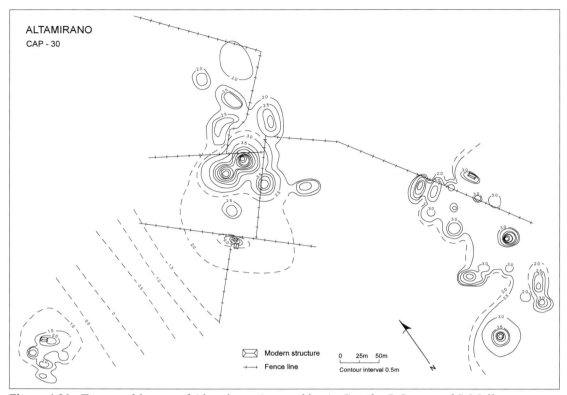

Figure 4.20. Topographic map of Altamirano (mapped by A. Gerstle, S. Levy, and J. Mallory; drafted by A. Nethery).

of the site, with lower, smaller mounds located toward the site periphery. These latter mounds are presumably house platforms. The site layout resembles the site plans at Acapetahua and Las Lomas, but the public mounds are not arranged in straight rows as in the other two sites.

Approximately 300 m west of the tallest mound on a hill that has not been mapped, we discovered several rock cairns that appear to be graves. These are similar to the ones that were observed at Las Campanitas. We assume that the graves date to sometime within the historic period but have no direct evidence concerning their age.

Rancho Novillero was occupied from the beginning of the Protoclassic period through the Late Classic period.

Rancho Retiro (CAP-75)

Rancho Retiro is located off the road to Limoncito, approximately 7 km in a straight line south of Bonanza. It is situated on flat terrain near a seasonal stream. Two tall conical mounds, the highest of which is 4.0 m, face each other at the site center. They form the sides of an open plaza, which has a ball court at the northern side. Another ball court is adjacent to the first one but perpendicular to it. The site is 13.46 ha, within which we have mapped 31 mounds (Figure 4.22).

The site was occupied from the beginning of the Protoclassic period through the Late Classic period, with its most intense occupation, as judged from surface ceramics, during the Middle to Late Classic periods.

Lomas López (CAP-56)

The small site of Lomas López is located south of Acapetahua, on the west side of the road to Matamoros. It is situated on flat terrain. The site measures 2.05 ha, within which we have mapped six platform mounds (Figure 4.23). One

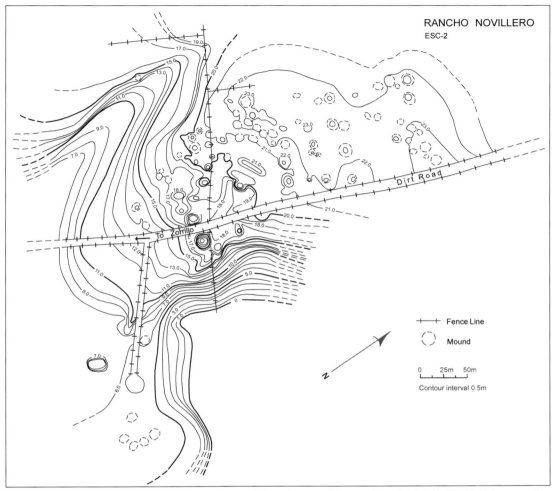

Figure 4.21. Topographic map of Rancho Novillero (mapped by A. Gerstle, M. Jaffe, K. Kiper, and S. Levy; drafted by A. Nethery).

of these is a tall (3.5 m) conical mound. All the others are large but low in elevation. The six mounds form two groups but the site layout is informal.

The results of our analysis of surface sherds indicate that the site was occupied from the beginning of the Protoclassic through the Late Classic period. A lighter occupation occurred during the Late Postclassic period.

Flor de Carmen (CAC-3)

Flor de Carmen is located on the upper coastal plain between Colonia Bonanza and

Colonia Soconusco, approximately 500 m east of the rail line. The site was first identified during the project reported here and was shown to Voorhies by a local informant.

This is a small site measuring only 0.96 ha and containing six mounds (Figure 4.24). The highest of these is located at the eastern part of the site and is only 1.5 m above the adjacent ground level. The remaining mounds are low, and two are lower than the 0.5 m chosen as the contour interval for the map.

Some of the recovered sherds from the site were coarse and plain, suggesting a domestic function. In addition, the crew recovered two

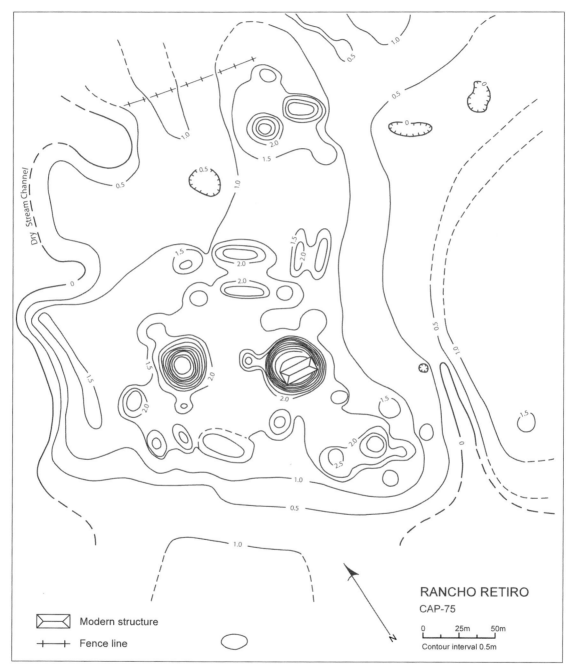

Figure 4.22. Topographic map of Rancho Retiro (mapped by M. Jaffe and B. Voorhies; drafted by A. Nethery).

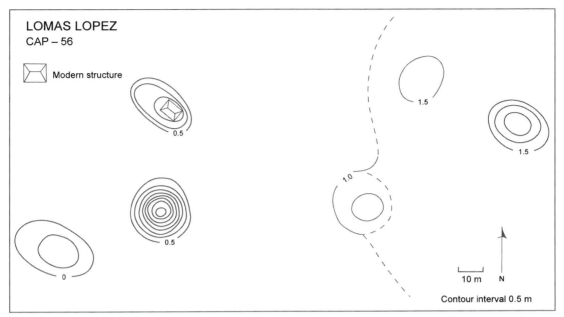

Figure 4.23. Topographic map of Lomas López (sketch map by A. Gerstle, M. Jaffe and J. Mallory; drafted by A. Nethery).

grinding stones (1 mano and 1 pestle) that support the same inference.

The site was occupied from the Protoclassic through the Late Classic, with a less intense occupation in the Late Postclassic period.

Loma Bonita (CAP-31)

Loma Bonita is located on lower portion of the coastal plain, approximately 17 km directly south of the rail line where it crosses the Río Cintalapa. The site appears on Navarrete's survey map (NWAF map archives).

It measures 5.92 ha and has 28 platform mounds (Figure 4.25). The highest mound is now 1.5 m above level ground but it has been lowered, perhaps by as much as a meter, by cattle that are penned in a corral on it. Five low mounds closely surround the tall conical mound. Other low mounds, east of the tallest one, surround an open area that appears to be a planned plaza.

According to our analysis of surface-collected sherds the site was occupied from the Protoclassic through the Late Classic periods, and in the Late Postclassic period. The study of

sherds indicates that occupation was substantial during both of these spans of time. The site plan, however, looks typically Classic so we describe the site in this section of the report.

La Islona (CAP-9)

La Islona was first identified by Carlos Navarrete (NWAF map archives). It is located within the wetlands, south of La Palma on an inactive barrier beach island. The 40 ha island is known locally as La Islona, but its official name may have been changed to Isla de San Antonio.

The site is only 3.91 ha in area, at least as we were able to define it at the time of the survey. It consists of five mounds, one of which is a tall, steep-sided conical mound that stands 10.5 m above the level ground (Figure 4.26). This is one of the largest platform constructions that we recorded in the study area; the only similar one in size is located at Los Carlos, an inland site.

The site plan (Figure 4.27) shows that there are two low mounds at the base of the high mound. Two other mounds are located to the northeast and northwest. There may be other

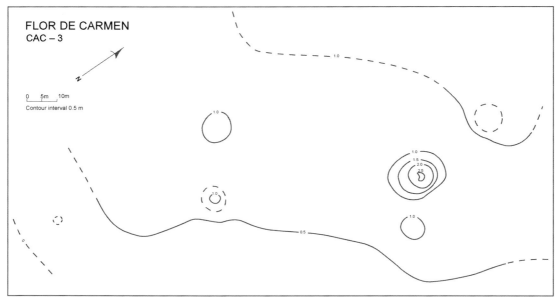

Figure 4.24. Topographic map of Flor de Carmen (mapped by J. Gasco; drafted by A. Nethery).

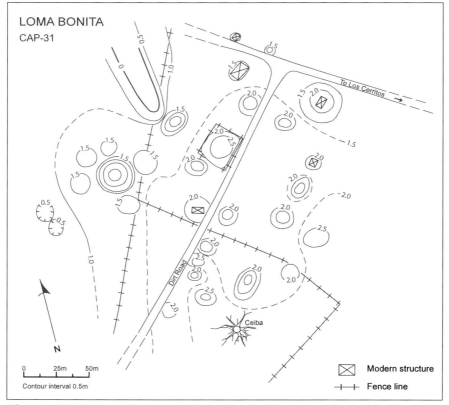

Figure 4.25. Topographic map of Loma Bonita (sketch map by A. Gerstle,
M. Jaffe, K. Kiper and J. Mallory; drafted by A. Nethery).

Figure 4.26. Photograph of largest mound at La Islona.

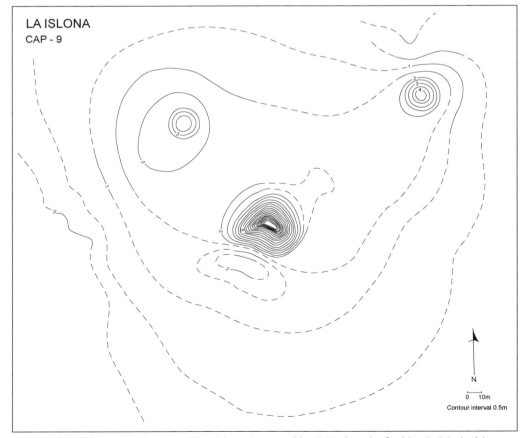

Figure 4.27. Topographic map of La Islona (mapped by J. Kules; drafted by S. Medaris).

low mounds in the vicinity of those shown on the map. At the time of mapping the site was covered with dense grass that made visibility very difficult.

The site was occupied during the Early to Late Classic periods according to our analysis of ceramics from the site surface. Also observed on the site surface were fragments of shell and obsidian. Pieces of human bone were recovered from the backdirt of a water well.

Lomas de Carrizal (CAP-10)

The Lomas de Carrizal site is located on the lower gradient of the coastal plain at the northern edge of a small lagoon within the seasonally inundated palm marsh formation. The site was identified from aerial photographs and verified in the field by Voorhies in 1978. Lomas de Carrizal consists of three mounds that provide dry land during the rainy season when the surrounding ground is inundated (Figure 4.28). The height of the tallest mound is 2.5 m. The site measures 1.11 ha.

Sherds were scarce on the surface of the site but our analysis of the small sample of diagnostic ceramics dates the site to the Early to Late Classic periods. This makes the site contemporaneous with nearby Río Arriba (Pfeiffer 1983; 1989).

Lomas César (CAP-29)

The Lomas César site is located southwest of Bonanza, approximately 7.5 km south of the Pan American Highway on the road to Santa Elena. It is located on flat, poorly drained terrain typical of the middle coastal plain. The mounds are situated on the highest ground of the locality. The site was discovered by casual rather than systematic survey.

We found 21 mounds in an area measuring 4.97 ha. The highest mound at the site (> 3.0 m) is at the east side of the mapped area (Figure 4.29). There is an open area to the west of this tall mound but no formal delineation of a plaza. A ball court is southwest of the tall mound.

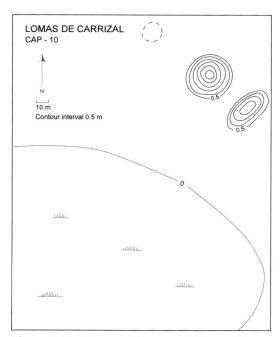

Figure 4.28. Topographic map of Lomas de Carrizal (survey with level, tape, and compass by J. Mallory; drafted by A. Nethery).

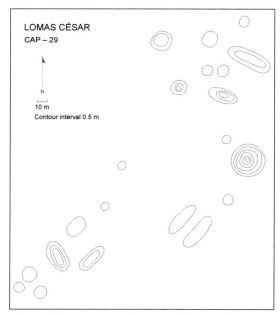

Figure 4.29. Topograpic map of Lomas César (sketch map by D. Hosler and J. Mallory; drafted by A. Nethery).

Dating is uncertain for this site, but we have tentatively placed it in the Early to Late Classic periods.

Río Arriba (CAP-32)

The Río Arriba site is located at the interface between the wetlands and the seasonally inundated zone. It is also located on the west bank of the Río Arriba where it enters mangrove-lined waterways. Accordingly, the inhabitants of the site are in close proximity to the palm marsh and mangrove formations, as well as the river and, farther inland, terra firma. Carlos Navarrete reported the site during his survey (NWAF map archives).

We mapped and collected artifacts from the surface during the first field season of Proyecto Soconusco. The site measures 7.2 ha, within

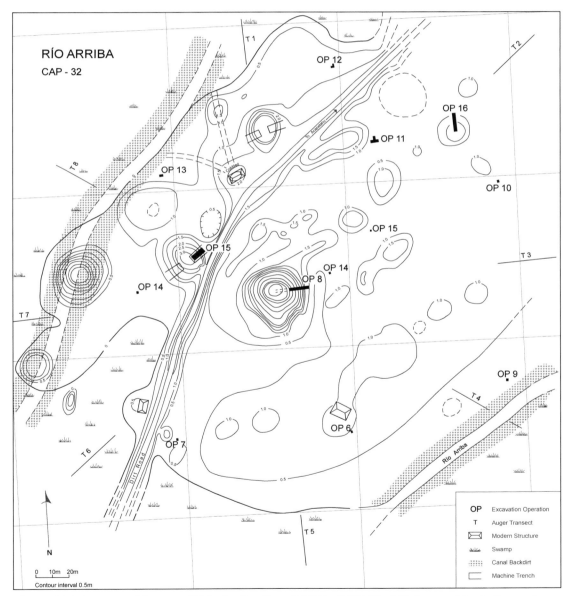

Figure 4.30. Topographic map of Río Arriba; from Pfeiffer (1989:Fig.6.2) (mapped by J. Gasco, L. Pfeiffer and D. Hosler; drafted by A. Nethery and L. Pfeiffer).

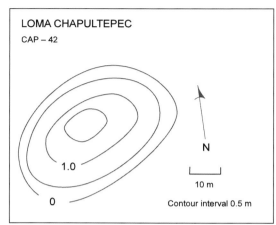

Figure 4.31. Topographic map of Loma Chapultepec (surveyed with level, tape, and compass by A. Gerstle; drafted by A. Nethery).

which we mapped 35 mounds (Figure 4.30). The highest mound (> 5.5 m) at the site is located approximately in the geographic center. This is a steep-sided conical mound that probably was the platform of a small temple, judging from its resemblance to other constructions in Mesoamerica. Other large, low mounds at the site appear to be aligned in rows. There does not seem to be a formally delineated plaza.

Surface sherds were exceptionally abundant at this site in comparison with others in our study area. During the first field season the crew collected approximately 2600 sherds, which constituted 22 percent of the season's entire collection (Pfeiffer 1989:158). Sherds were denser on the surfaces of mounds compared with the areas between mounds. This might have been the result of the heavier pedestrian traffic on the mounds, many of which had been recently become house sites at the time of our survey. Still, the number of sherds and the diversity of sherd types did not seem to be explained fully by the recent history of the site. We speculated that it might have been a production center for pottery and/or a depot for pottery being transported via the waterways.

Linda Pfeiffer, then a graduate student at University of California-Santa Barbara, decided to investigate the question of the function of this

site as her doctoral research. Her investigations are reported in her dissertation and elsewhere (Pfeiffer 1983; 1989). She determined conclusively that Río Arriba had been a pottery-making community during the Classic period. Pfeiffer discovered the archaeological remains of pottery-manufacturing activity areas in the excavations and paste analyses of both potsherds and local clays demonstrated that the vessels had been manufactured locally.

Río Arriba was occupied continuously from the Early Classic through the Late Classic periods. Neff (1984), who analyzed Plumbate sherds from the site, found that some sherds were made of the Tohil paste, which dates to the Early Postclassic period.

This once lovely archaeological site is now totally destroyed due to the activities of its current inhabitants.

Loma Chapultepec (CAP-42)

This is a large, isolated mound (Figure 4.31) located close to the seasonally inundated zone on the lower coastal plain. It is northeast of Laguna Los Cerritos. The site area is 0.7 ha and the mound is 1.5 m high.

This mound may have formed through gradual accumulation of debris rather than being an intentionally constructed platform mound; however, we have no evidence that addresses the formation processes at the site. It dates to the Early Classic through Late Classic periods.

Garrapata (CAP-43)

Garrapata is located approximately 1 km southeast of Loma Chapultepec and is similarly close to the seasonally inundated portion of the study area. It consists of a single, large mound (Figure 4.32), in this case adjacent to an *aguada*. The site measures 0.42 ha and the mound is 2.5 m high but poorly defined at the base. We are unsure whether the site formed through the accumulation of debris or whether it was intentionally constructed as a platform mound. It was occupied from the Early Classic through Late Classic periods.

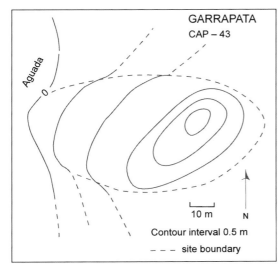

Figure 4.32. Topographic map of Garrapata (sketch map by A. Gerstle; drafted by A. Nethery).

Lomas Perdidas (CAP-44)

This site is south of Matamoros and is situated on flat terrain. It is a small site (1.65 ha) with only eight platform mounds (Figure 4.33). The highest mound has an elevation of 1.0 m, but it is not strikingly taller than other mounds at the site. The site has been plowed, however, so it is probable that the mounds have been lowered by this practice. Given its appearance, we interpret this as a cluster of residential mounds rather than a public center.

The site was in use from the Early to Late Classic periods.

Lomas Plátano (CAP-45)

Lomas Plátano is located south of Matamoros, on flat terrain. It consists of two coalescing platform mounds (Figure 4.34). The higher mound is now a meter in elevation, but

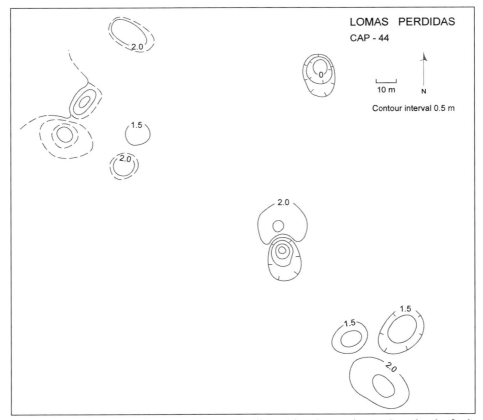

Figure 4.33. Topographic map of Lomas Perdidas (sketch map by A. Gerstle; drafted by A. Nethery).

plowing is now carried out at the site so these two mounds may have been higher in the past. The site area is 0.24 ha.

The occupation was during the Early to Late Classic periods as determined from surface ceramics.

Lomas Tránsito (CAP-53)

Lomas Tránsito is located on the road to Matamoros, which cuts through the site (Figure 4.34). The terrain is flat, and the site was covered by a cacao grove at the time of our investigations. The site measures 5.96 ha, within which we have mapped 19 mounds. The tallest of these is 3.5 m high. It may form one side of an open plaza area, but the road cut passes just at this point so it is impossible to tell. A probable ball court is at the northwest edge of the site but it is highly eroded.

The site was occupied from the Early to Late Classic periods, according to our analysis of the rather small collection of surface sherds.

Rancho Haig (CAP-58)

Rancho Haig is located near the road between Acapetahua and Río Arriba, about 2 km north of Luis Espinosa. This small site (0.80 ha) is situated on flat terrain. It has five mounds, the highest of which is two meters (Figure 4.35). The mounds form an arc with an open space in the center. This may be a residential, rather than public site.

The site was occupied from the Early to Late Classic periods.

Rancho San Juan (CAP-63)

Rancho San Juan is located on Transect E-17 (Figure 1.16), near the road that connects Acacoyagua with Matamoros. The site is situated on a small hill. It has a least 14 mounds, only 11 of which are shown on the map. The map was not finished because the ranch owner withdrew access permission (given originally by the ranch manager) from the mapping crew before the map was completed. The owner felt

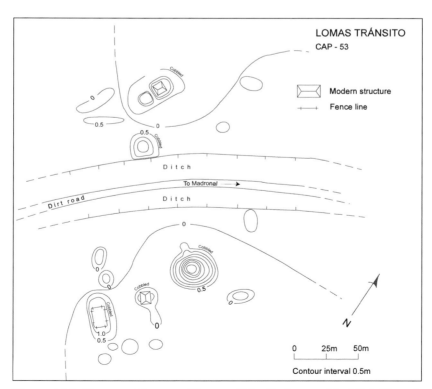

Figure 4.34. Topographic map of Lomas Tránsito (mapped by M. Jaffe and B. Voorhies; drafted by A. Nethery).

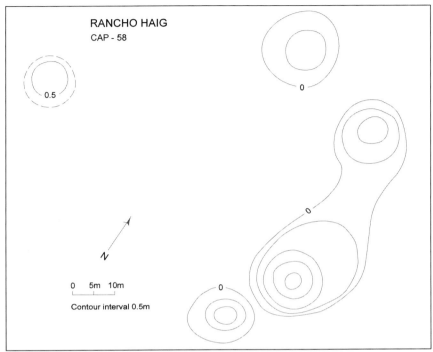

Figure 4.35. Topographic map of Rancho Haig (sketch mapped by J. Mallory; drafted by A. Nethery).

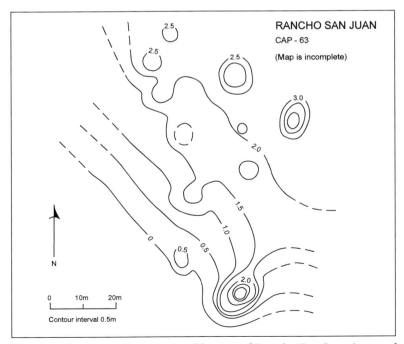

Figure 4.36. Incomplete topographic map of Rancho San Juan (mapped by M. Jaffe and J. Mallory; drafted by A. Nethery).

that our presence might exacerbate a preexisting land dispute.

The site measures at least 0.65 ha within which we mapped the 11 mounds (Figure 4.36). The highest mound is 1.5 m above the ground level on its northern side but is steeper to the south. This mound and several others have cobbles eroding from the surfaces, indicating that they have stone facings. The site layout is informal in that the mounds do not form any evident pattern.

The site was occupied from the Early Classic through the Late Classic periods according to our analysis of surface sherds.

Salto de Agua (CAP-65)

The site of Salto de Agua is a cluster of graves situated on top of a hill overlooking the coastal plain. The site is located northeast of the Colombia rail station. The site was not mapped, but we counted a minimum of ten rock cairns that appear to be graves in an area of approximately 900 m². We presume that this cemetery is historic in age for the same reasons discussed for the graves at Las Campanitas; however, the few sherds from the site date from the Early to Late Classic periods. For this reason the site is included on the regional map (Figure 4.1) and chronology chart (Figure 1.5).

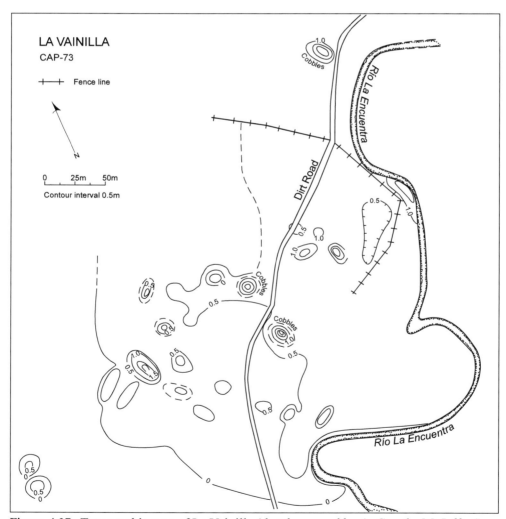

Figure 4.37. Topographic map of La Vainilla (sketch mapped by A. Gerstle, M. Jaffe, S. Levy, and B. Voorhies; drafted by A. Nethery).

La Vainilla (CAP-73)

La Vainilla is located southwest of Colonia Soconusco, on flat land where distributaries of the Río Jalapa thread across the terrain. The site is next to the Río La Encuentra, one of these distributaries (Figure 4.37). The site covers an area of 10.25 ha, within which we have mapped 25 mounds. There is a circular cluster of large mounds that surrounds a plaza in the southeastern portion of the site. A ball court and the tallest mound at the site (> 2.0 m) are part of this group. Some of these mounds appear to be aligned in rows, but this may not have been the original intent. Some of the larger mounds have cobbles eroding from their surfaces, indicating that the platforms are rock faced.

We had difficulty finding surface sherds at this site. The few diagnostic ones that we recovered date between the Early and Late Classic periods, but this site is not dated firmly.

Las Lomitas (CAP-74)

Las Lomitas is located south of Sesecapa on the lower gradient of the coastal plain. The terrain is flat but fairly well drained. Although it is not within the zone that floods seasonally on a regular basis, flooding can be a problem at the site. The site is near a stream channel that carries water during the wet season.

The area of Las Lomitas measures 8.22 ha, within which we have identified 19 mounds (Figure 4.38). The highest mound is 3 m in

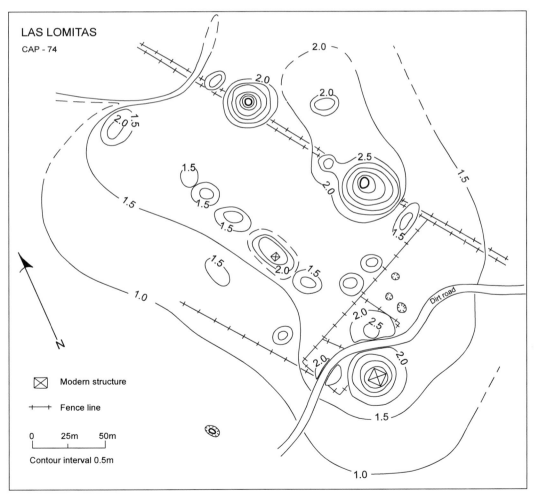

Figure 4.38. Topographic map of Las Lomitas (mapped by M. Jaffe and S. Levy; drafted by A. Nethery).

elevation. It forms part of the boundary of a rectangular plaza. The west side of the plaza is limited by an alignment of five closely spaced mounds that resemble the alignments at Acapetahua.

Dating is uncertain because only a few sherds were recovered from the site surface and many were not diagnostic. We have placed the occupation from the Early Classic through the Late Classic primarily on the basis of site plan.

Rancho Abandonado (CAP-76)

Rancho Abandonado is located a short distance northeast of Río Arriba and adjacent to the road leading from Luis Espinoza to Río Arriba. It is well within the seasonally inundated zone.

The site consists of a single mound (Figure 4.39) that measures 0.09 ha in area. It is approximately 3 m high. During reconnaissance we did not find any surface sherds that would permit the dating of the site. However, Linda Pfeiffer revisited the site during her study of

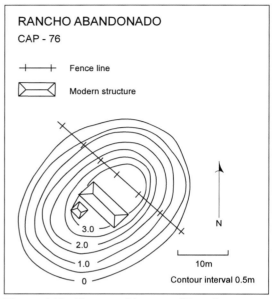

Figure 4.39. Topographic map of Rancho Abandonado (surveyed with pace and compass, height estimated, by B. Voorhies; drafted by A. Nethery).

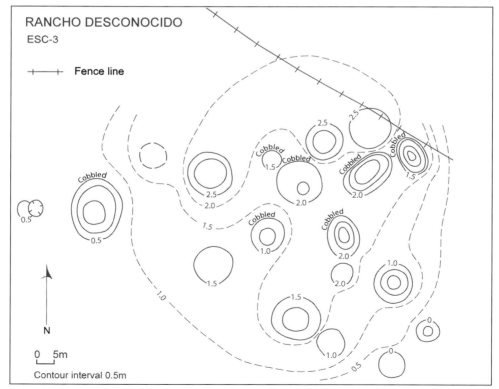

Figure 4.40. Topographic map of Rancho Desconocido (sketch mapped by S. Levy and J. Mallory; drafted by A. Nethery).

Río Arriba (Pfeiffer 1983) and was able to collect some sherds at that time. She places the occupation during the entire Early to Late Classic time span.

Rancho Desconocido (ESC-3)

Rancho Desconocido is located on terra firma, close to the road connecting Route 200 with the rail station at Colombia. The site covers 0.94 ha, within which we have located 19 mounds (Figure 4.40). The tallest mound, which is relatively conical, is 2 m high. It is located west of the other mounds that we mapped. No formal arrangement of the remaining mounds is discernible to us.

The site was occupied during the Early to Late Classic periods, as dated from ceramics collected from its surface.

Campo Jerónimo (COM-2)

This is a large isolated mound located a short distance east of Río Arriba. Although not within the strictly defined seasonally inundated zone, it is on the lower elevation of the coastal plain that is subject to occasional flooding. The mound measures 0.10 ha and is 3 m high (Figure 4.41). It is not entirely clear whether this mound is an intentional platform construction or if it formed through the accumulation of debris.

We place the occupation from the Early to Late Classic periods on the basis of a limited quantity of sherds collected from the site surface.

Guardanía (COM-3)

Guardanía is located near the eastern boundary of our study area, approximately 4 km south of Colonia Hidalgo. In this area the terrain is flat and flooding can be a problem.

The site is small, measuring only 0.68 ha, within which we have identified five mounds (Figure 4.42). This site has been disturbed heavily by machinery, so it is probable that additional mounds have been "erased." A local informant reported that formerly there were more low mounds than were visible at the time of our visit. The highest extant mound stands 3 m, and this may not have been lowered significantly by machinery as the surface

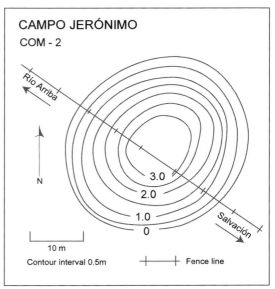

Figure 4.41. Topographic map of Campo Jerónimo (surveyed with pace and compass, height estimated, by B. Voorhies; drafted by A. Nethery).

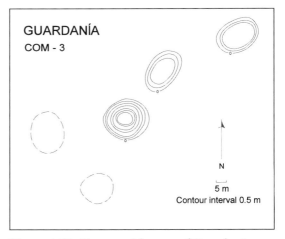

Figure 4.42. Topographic map of Guardanía (sketch mapped by B. Voorhies; drafted by A. Nethery).

appears undisturbed. All that may be said about the site plan is that the highest mound is centrally situated.

We place the site occupation from the Early to Late Classic periods on the basis of surface ceramics.

La Unión (COM-5)

La Unión is located near the road that connects Colonia Hidalgo with Salvación. The terrain is flat and featureless at this location. The site consists of a scattering of sherds in a banana orchard, but according to the owner of the property a low mound had been present previously before it was destroyed by modern agricultural activities.

We were unable to map the site for lack of surface features, but it is probable that it was a small residential mound, judging from its description. The sherds collected indicate that the site was occupied throughout the Classic Period.

Cruz de Piedra (CAC-8)

Cruz de Piedra is situated on two adjacent hilltops, located east of the road connecting Colonia Soconusco with Route 200. Voorhies found the site while traveling in the study area, but it was also within Transect E-17 (Figure 1.16). The site provides an excellent vantage point overlooking the coastal plain, the Río Jalapa, and the piedmont of the coastal range.

The site area is large, 16.96 ha, because we included the mounds on two adjacent hills despite the fact that no mounds were found in the wide, intervening gullies (Figure 4.43). Three small, cobble-faced mounds were mapped, and a rock scatter suggests the possible former presence of a fourth mound.

Given the hilltop situation of these mounds, we would expect a Late Postclassic period occupation, but only a Classic period occupation was indicated by the analysis of surface sherds. It is noteworthy that only a few diagnostic sherds were recovered, so a later occupation cannot be discounted at the present time.

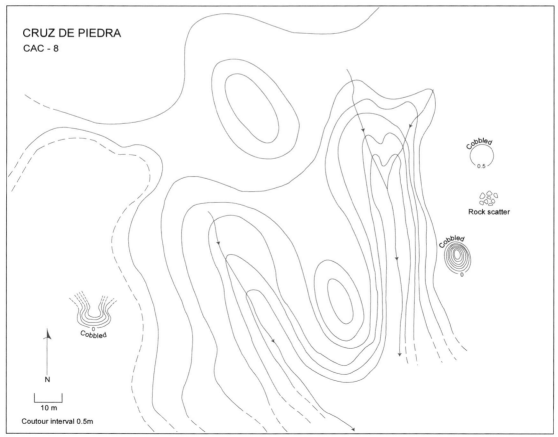

Figure 4.43. Topographic map of Cruz de Piedra (sketch mapped by B. Voorhies; drafted by A. Nethery).

Coquito (CAP-21)

This platform mound site was occupied during the Protoclassic through Late Classic periods and again during the Late Postclassic period. It has been described previously by Voorhies and Gasco (2004:58-59), together with the nearby site of Coquito 2 (CAP-22). We discuss these two sites in the chapter on the Late Postclassic period (Chapter 5).

Loma Cacao (CAP-68)

Loma Cacao is a small, isolated platform mound located approximately 2 km south of Colonia Soconusco. The terrain is flat in the vicinity of the site. The site measures 0.06 ha, with the single mound reaching a height of 1 m (Figure 4.44). An informant told us that there are three mounds at this site, but we only found the one that appears on the map.

The site had been plowed, and sherds were fairly abundant on the site surface at the time of our visit. Using these we have established the site occupation to within the Classic period, with a less intense occupation during the Late Postclassic period.

Lomas de Piedra (CAP-11)

The site Lomas de Piedra is located on the road connecting Bonanza (Colonia Ejidal Jiquilpan) with Ranchería Santa Elena, about 3.5 km southwest of the rail line. A local informant described the site to Voorhies. The site is situated on flat terrain.

The most striking feature about the site is that the surface of the tallest mound (5.5 m high) is thickly strewn with rocks. This is, of course, the reason for the site name. Some of the surface rocks on this mound are river cobbles, such as were used widely for retaining walls at many other sites within the study area. More unusual are the abundant tabular slabs of a metamorphic rock, probably a banded gneiss. These rocks apparently were used as facing and are probably locally available, but we do not know their exact source.

Mounds between 0.5 and 1.0 m high surround the tallest mound (Figure 4.45). These exhibit no regular orientation and the site plan is informal. Many have cobbles eroding

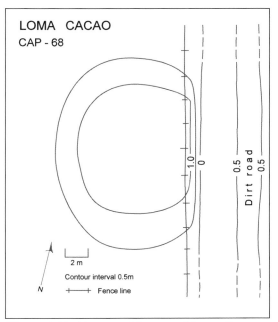

Figure 4.44. Topographic map of Loma Cacao (surveyed with level, tape, and compass by A. Gerstle; drafted by A. Nethery).

from their surfaces, so they too probably had stone retaining walls. Mounds also were found at considerable distances from the primary group. These mounds occur singly and in small clusters. One distinct mound cluster is situated at the northwestern periphery of the site. One of these mounds has cobbles visibly eroding from its surface.

As currently defined, the site is very large in extent; it measures 56.66 ha. Fifty-eight mounds were mapped. This site was in pasture when we mapped it, and perhaps because of the excellent visibility, we were able to find many more low mounds than at other sites. The large spatial area covered by the site compared to other sites in the sample is probably due to this unusually good visibility.

Surface artifacts were scarce when we mapped and surface collected the site. We observed many fragments of slab-legged metates and a single mano fragment. According to the results of the analysis of sherds from the surface, the site was occupied throughout the Classic period and again in the Late Postclassic period.

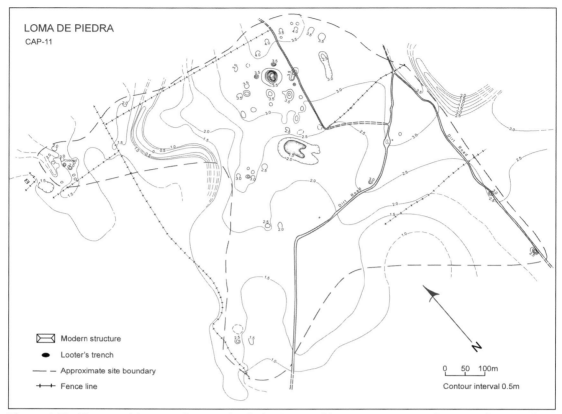

Figure 4.45. Topographic map of Loma de Piedra (mapped by J. Gasco, D. Hosler, J. Mallory, and L. Pfeiffer; drafted by A. Nethery).

We have difficulty identifying the primary occupation of the site but are considering it together with other Classic period sites because the site plan seems to be typical of the Classic period rather than the Late Postclassic period.

Rancho San Marcos (CAP-34)

Rancho San Marcos is located on the west side of the road that connects Acacoyagua with the rail line. The site is situated on top of a low hill, but the topography is not shown on our planimetric sketch map (Figure 4.46). We identified four mounds within an area measuring 0.30 ha. The highest mound is 3.0 m in elevation and is located north of the other three mounds.

The site was occupied during the Middle through Late Classic periods.

Lomas Frijoles (CAP-57)

Lomas Frijoles is located near the road that connects Acacoyagua with Matamoros. It is approximately 1 km south of the rail line. The site, consisting of only two mounds, is situated on flat terrain. One of these has an unusual rectangular outline (Figure 4.47) but this is due to modern modification as the platform supported a building until very recently.

The site measures 0.39 ha and the tallest mound is only 1 m high. The two mounds are close to one another and probably are platforms that once supported domestic structures.

On the basis of surface sherds we date the site to the Middle through Late Classic periods.

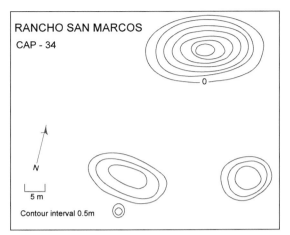

Figure 4.46. Topographic map of Rancho San Marcos (sketch mapped by J. Mallory; drafted by A. Nethery).

Loma Grande (CAP-72)

Loma Grande is located on Transect B-2 (Figure 1.8), approximately 1.75 km north of Santa Elena. The terrain is flat in the vicinity of the site, but a river channel that holds water seasonally borders the site. The site consists of a single mound and a nearby depression (Figure 4.48). The site area measures 0.38 ha, and the mound is 1.0 m in elevation.

The site was occupied during the Middle to Late Classic periods according to the analysis of sherds collected from its surface.

Santa Elena #2 (MAP-1)

Santa Elena #2 is located south of Sesecapa, about midway between the northern and southern limits of the study area. It is situated on flat terrain next to a swamp that contained water in January 1979 when the site was visited. The site is 2.71 ha in area, within which we have mapped 15 low mounds, the highest of which is only a meter in elevation (Figure 4.49). Some mounds form a semicircle that opens onto the swamp. Other mounds have no discernible pattern.

This site was occupied during the Middle to Late Classic periods according to our analysis of the surface sherds.

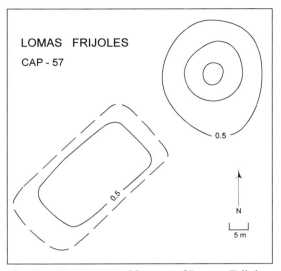

Figure 4.47. Topographic map of Lomas Frijoles (sketch mapped by A. Gerstle and M. Jaffe; drafted by A. Nethery).

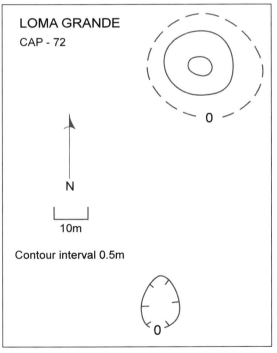

Figure 4.48. Topographic map of Loma Grande (sketch mapped by J. Mallory; drafted by A. Nethery).

Doña María (CAP-67)

Doña María is located south of Colonia Soconusco near the middle of the study area. The site is plotted on Navarrete's survey map (NWAF map archives). The terrain is flat in the general vicinity of the site. The site consists of seven platform mounds in an area measuring 3.36 ha. The mounds are aligned roughly along a north-south axis (Figure 4.50), with the tallest mound at the southern end. This mound stands 2.0 m above the adjacent ground level.

We had intended to test this site during the second field season, but it had been leveled by plowing and planted densely in banana plants when we returned. We were able to collect abundant surface material that indicates that the site was occupied during the Early to Late Classic periods.

Loma Eduardo (CAP-52)

Loma Eduardo is an isolated mound located near the road that connects Acapetahua with Las Garzas. It is approximately 2 km south of the

rail line and situated on flat terrain. The single mound that constitutes the site measures 0.11 ha and is only one meter high (Figure 4.51).

The site was occupied during the Late Classic and Late Postclassic periods. The mound probably supported a domestic structure during both time periods. We have arbitrarily chosen to include this brief description in the present chapter rather than in the chapter on Postclassic period sites.

INTRASITE SETTLEMENT PATTERNS AND BURIAL PATTERNS

As we mentioned in the introduction to this chapter, we have 47 sites in our inventory with terminal occupations during the Late Classic period. We now turn to an analysis of the intrasite layouts of these sites in order to detect any regularities in site patterning that might shed light on the sociopolitical organization of the population at that time.

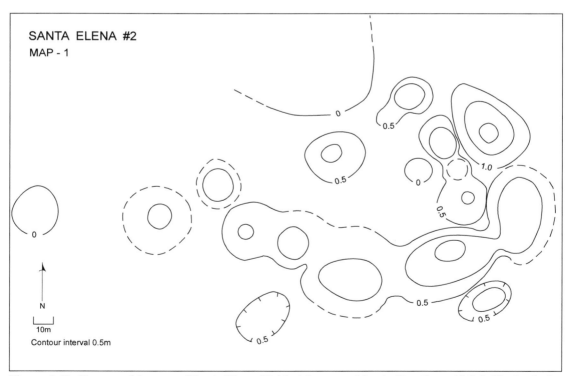

Figure 4.49. Topographic map of Santa Elena #2 (sketch mapped by A. Gerstle and M. Jaffe; drafted by A. Nethery).

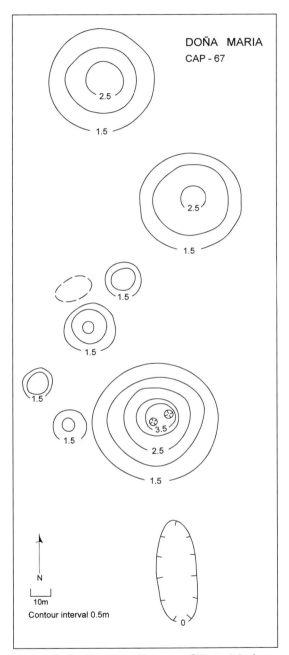

Figure 4.50. Topographic map of Doña Maria (sketch mapped by M. Jaffe, K. Kiper, and S. Levy; drafted by A. Nethery).

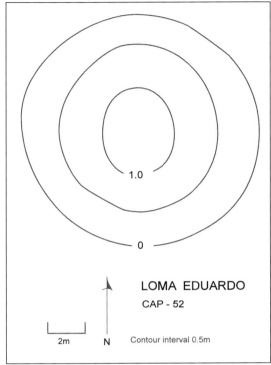

Figure 4.51. Topographic map of Loma Eduardo (surveyed with pace and compass, height estimated, by B. Voorhies; drafted by A. Nethery).

The first group consists of sites with a minimal number of mounds that are not architecturally differentiated. We suspect that these sites are strictly residential in function. Seven of these sites consist of one mound only: Loma Chapultepec (CAP-42), Garrapata (CAP-43), Rancho Abandonado (CAP-76), Campo Jerónimo (COM-2), Loma Cacao (CAP-68), Loma Grande (CAP-72), and Loma Eduardo (CAP-52). The placement of Rancho Abandonado and Campo Jerónimo in this group may be misleading, however, since each of their single mounds is over 3 m above the surrounding ground level. This suggests a more substantial construction effort than in the other sites of the group. The remaining sites in the group have two (Lomas Gutiérrez [CAP-69], Loma Plátano [CAP-45], and Lomas Frijoles [CAP-57]) or more mounds (Flor de Carmen

[CAC-3], Lomas de Carrizal [CAP-10], Lomas Perdidas [CAP-44], Rancho Haig [CAP-58], Rancho Desconocido [ESC-3], Rancho San Marcos [CAP-34], and Santa Elena #2 [MAP-1]).

The second group of Late Classic period sites that we have identified consists of sites with one or more tall conical mounds, numerous low, flat-topped mounds but no ball courts. The sites we have placed in this category are Las Campanitas (CAC-6), Herrado (CAP-5), Lomas López (CAP-56), Loma Bonita (CAP-31), La Islona (CAP-9), Las Lomitas (CAP-74), La Concepción (CAP-24), Dos Amates (CAC-2), Río Arriba (CAP-32), Loma de Piedra (CAP-11), Guardanía (COM-3), Doña Maria (CAP-67), and Rancho San Juan (CAP-63). We see no uniformity in site patterning, with the exception that most sites appear to have an open space in the vicinity of the tall conical mound. We speculate that these open spaces were created for public performances of some unknown nature. Accordingly, we assume that the conical mound plus adjacent open space are the architectural focal points for community-wide activities. In some cases, such as in Loma Bonita and Las Lomitas, the mounds are aligned in such a way that a rectangular space is created that could be characterized as a formal plaza. The boundary of the open space is not rectilinear at some of the other sites, for example at Dos Amates. In these cases the open space is informally defined. Finally, in some instances, such as at Doña María, we did not detect an open space in the vicinity of the tall conical mound. We do not know if the original site plan lacked an open space or whether it formerly existed but was destroyed.

Our third group consists of sites with one or more tall conical mounds, numerous low flat-topped mounds, and one or more ball courts. In this group, we have placed Campíto (CAP-15), Nicolás Bravo (MAP-4), Rancho Alegre (CAP-55), Los Descansados (CAP-66), Las Lomas (COM-6), El Conchal (CAP-14), Acapetahua (CAP-1), Altamirano (CAP-30, Rancho Novillero (ESC-2), Rancho Retiro (CAP-75), Lomas César (CAP-29), Lomas Tránsito (CAP-53), and La Vainilla (CAP-73). The site plans resemble those in the second group in that some

have open spaces near the conical mound that are rectangular in shape, whereas others are more irregular in outline. The ball courts are always near the highest mound at the site and are often at the opposite side from it across the open space. This tendency is not invariant, however.

Finally, there are two sites that do not fit the classification system offered above. La Cancha (CAP-50) is unique in that it has a ball court but no tall conical mound. We suspect that such a mound once was present but has been destroyed, but we have no firm evidence of this. Also, Cruz de Piedra (CAC-8) seems highly unusual. Although it has only three mounds, two of these are not as broad and flat-topped as most mounds that we suspect were house platforms. Its hilltop location and the two steep-sided mounds suggest to us that its function in prehistoric times was different from the other sites considered here. For this reason we have set it aside in the present analysis.

In summary, our examination of site maps pertaining to the Late Classic period has led us to propose that during this time period there were small presumably residential sites scattered over the landscape. These are likely household clusters for families of various sizes depending on life cycle and other fortunes. The larger settlements all have public/communal areas with two key architectural features, open spaces and tall, conical platform mounds. Moreover, some of these sites have ball courts associated with the other public features. Other than the presence of a public/communal area there is little regularity in architectural layout that we have been able to detect. This suggests to us that the residents of these sites probably were not integrated into any large, dominant sociopolitical sphere. In Chapter 6 we return again to the question of regional organization as reflected in these settlement data.

We now turn to the available data on human burials with the hope that they will shed additional light on the nature of Late Classic period society in the western Soconusco. We have only four burials dating to the Late Classic period, two children and two adults (Appendix A: Human Burials). Two of these burials are from Río Arriba, whereas one burial is from

Las Morenas and the other from Las Lomas. All the buried individuals were placed in simple pit graves in flat, non-mounded areas of their respective sites. The children lacked grave goods except for a piece of ochre on one child's foot. One of the adults also lacked grave goods. The other adult, a mature male from Las Morenas, was accompanied in death by a spherical spindle whorl and an unslipped, utilitarian bowl. This individual also had horizontal grooves at the root/crown junction of many of his teeth. Grooves such as these can be formed when the teeth are used during fiber working. In Mesoamerica, indications of fiber working are normally expected to be associated with female skeletal remains, but in this case Mary Hartman decided that the remains from Las Morenas were those of a male. This is intriguing and has led us to suspect that this man was making twine, most likely to be used for fishing equipment (lines or nets). The spindle whorl is fairly large (2.9 cm diameter; 2.5 cm in height) and heavy, which suggests that the yarn would be thick, as is the case with twine. Until the introduction of commercial twine in the early 20th century, local men made twine for their fishing nets from the fibers of wild *ixtle* (i.e., agave; Don Martín de los Santos, personal communication). It seems possible that the man buried at Las Morenas was using his teeth as a tool in this process.

Two of the four Late Classic period burials have evidence of physical trauma. The child from Las Lomas had lost part of a foot prior to death, whereas the mature adult male from Las Morenas had a lesion on the skull above the nuchal area. In addition, he was missing his femora and left tibia but otherwise the skeleton was complete and articulated. Although the burial sample is much too small for us to determine the overall health status of the population and degree of violence in its society,

these observations at least raise the possibility that social conditions were adverse by Late Classic times.

Our largest sample of human burials is from the Middle Classic period (n=13) so we will turn to these data in order to shed additional light on the well-being of the ancient people of the Soconusco. It should be noted that no sites were abandoned immediately at the end of the Middle Classic period, and for this reason we have not addressed intrasite settlement patterns for that period.

All the Middle Classic burials were interred in simple pits, and they range in age from infant to mature adult. In contrast to what we found for the Late Classic period, grave goods accompany all burials, with one exception, a young man from Las Lomas. One adult female at Río Arriba seems to have suffered a blow to the head, but this was the only recorded evidence of trauma in the studied population. The population also appears to have been healthy, except for a surprisingly high degree of tooth decay.

In summary, the burial data are too limited to make firm conclusions about the Soconusco population during the Late Classic period. Not only is the sample frustratingly small for this period, but also the excavators have not always provided sufficient detail to resolve questions of interpretation. Nonetheless, the data do allow for the following hypotheses to be advanced for further testing in the future.

Hypothesis 1: Health status declined in the Soconusco population over time between the Middle Classic and Late Classic periods.

Hypothesis 2: The incidence of violence increased over time between the Middle Classic and Late Classic periods.

Hypothesis 3: The distribution of durable goods became less equitable over time between the Middle Classic and Late Classic periods.

CHAPTER 5

SITES WITH FINAL, LATE POSTCLASSIC PERIOD OCCUPATIONS

SITE DESCRIPTIONS

There are 32 sites in our inventory with Late Postclassic period occupations (Voorhies 1989b:123; Fig. 5.1), but only 13 have substantial terminal occupations during this time period. Of these, four do not have platform mounds (Filapa, CAP-13; Zoológico, CAP-31; Ladrillo, CAP-12; and CAP-64) so they cannot be used to investigate the intrasite settlement patterns for the time period. These four sites are described in Appendix B: Miscellaneous Sites. The remaining nine sites have platform mounds and are presented here.

Acapetahua (CAP-1)

As we discussed in Chapter 4, the Acapetahua site lies immediately adjacent to the modern town of the same name and has two spatially separate public areas that we know from our subsurface investigations were constructed and abandoned at different times. The Classic center is situated on a floodplain, whereas the Postclassic center is situated on top of a long ridge. Details of our excavations upon which we base this summary may be found in Voorhies and Gasco (2004:14ff).

Our subsurface testing at the site showed that the top of the ridge was substantially modified during the Late Postclassic period, at which time it was leveled and platform mounds were constructed or remodeled. There are 55 mounds within the area that we consider the Late Postclassic period center of this multicomponent site (Figure 5.2). These include a few small, low mounds that are peripherally located and that may well be platforms for residences, but there are also larger mounds that must have had some type of public function. Among the monumental mounds are several tall, conical platform mounds. These mounds are much larger than any of the monumental

mounds located on the adjacent floodplain and that appear to have been constructed during the Classic period. For example, one of the conical mounds on the ridge is located at its southernmost end and is 5 m high, whereas twin platforms near the center of the ridge stand 6.5 and 7.5 m high. Figure 5.3 is a photograph of Mound 2, the lower of the paired mounds.

The twin conical platform mounds are striking because of their height, steep sides, and proximity to each other. We conjecture that these platform mounds once supported temples, and, if so, each may have been dedicated to a different deity, analogous to the situation at the Templo Mayor in Tenochtitlán where twin temples are dedicated to two principal deities. There, however, the temples surmount a single platform. The twin platforms at Acapetahua may delimit the southeastern boundary of a rectangular plaza group. At least there is a large flat area to their west, but platform mounds do not bound this area on all sides. Unfortunately, this area had dense vegetation when it was mapped, so we may have missed low mounds if they are present.

Nonetheless, at the north end of the main ridge there is a large, formal rectangular plaza that is bounded on its northwest side by a ball court and on the south by a long platform. We do not know if the plaza had a prepared surface, but a low circular platform made of cobbles was located in the plaza in front of the long platform. We were unable to determine the function of this feature, but its location suggests to us that this was the foundation of an altar or shrine. Such a function is consistent with similar structures throughout Mesoamerica. In addition, a broken, tabular stone now lies near the ballcourt and perhaps was once a painted stela. This is one of the few sites in the study area where there is surviving stone sculpture.

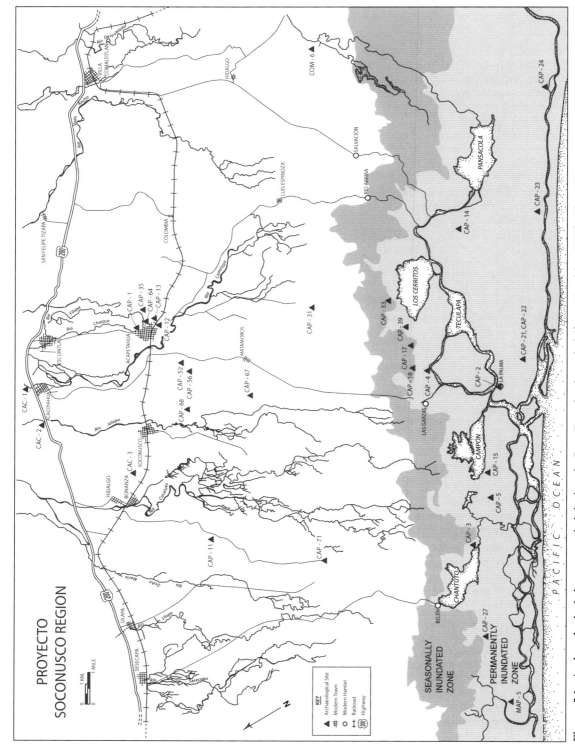

Figure 5.1. Archaeological sites occuppied during the Late Postclassic period (from Voorhies 1989b: Fig. 5.15).

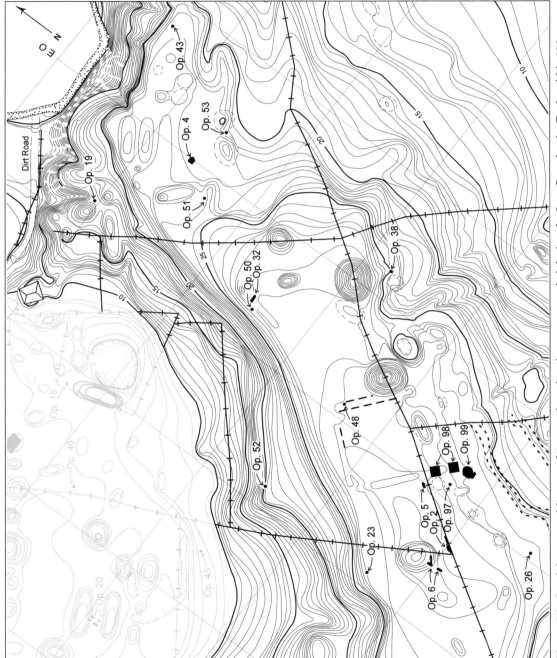

Figure 5.2. Partial topographic map of Acapetahua showing area occupied during the Last Postclassic. Each grid is 100 m on a side.

Figure 5.3.   Photograph of Mound 2, Acapetahua.

Another quadrilateral open space is immediately southwest of the twin platforms. It is defined by three exceptionally long, narrow mounds and on the southeast side by a shorter oblong mound. This is obviously another formally planned group of platforms that was constructed during the Late Postclassic period.

Farther to the west from the previously described plaza group there are other large mounds including the tall conical mound at the extreme western end of the ridge. At this part of the site, however, there are no clearly demarcated plaza groups.

While it appears certain that the public architecture of Acapetahua was centered on the ridge top during the Late Postclassic occupation, the town's residences were probably located in other places. In fact, we discovered the remains of one Late Postclassic period domestic residence on the floodplain where it overlay two other residences constructed in earlier times (Voorhies and Gasco 2004:36ff). The Late Postclassic period house was not raised

on a platform, but stone alignments mark the positions of the walls. The Late Postclassic period custom of building houses directly on the ground surface without constructing platforms makes it difficult for archaeologists to locate the positions of former houses because they become buried with sediments.

Ethnohistoric sources record the Aztec conquest of a town called Acapetlatlan, which later became a tributary within the Aztec Empire. There is compelling evidence that we have summarized elsewhere that the archaeological site is the same place as the town known from the written documents (Gasco and Voorhies 1989).

La Palma (CAP-2)

The archaeological site of La Palma is located within the wetlands on an inactive beach ridge that forms an island along one of the main canals in the estuary. The site's planimetric map shows 33 mounds in an area that measures 16.75 ha (Figure 5.4). Unfortunately, the site is

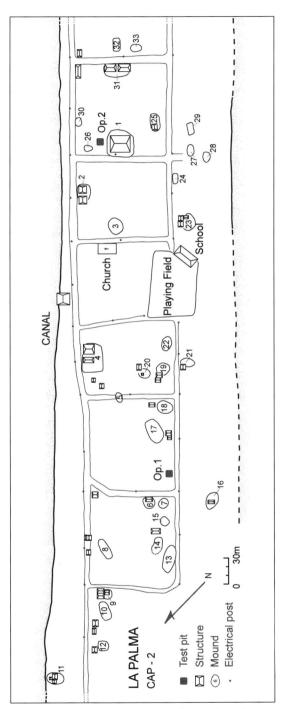

Figure 5.4.   Planimetric map of La Palma (pace and compass map by A. Bennett, J. Carpenter, B. Voorhies; drafted by S. Mederis).

currently the location of a fishing village and the mounds are heavily disturbed. Because of the substantial reduction in the height of the mounds, and the obstacles presented by modern constructions, we did not measure the height of the mounds when we mapped the site in 1983. Today the mounds are even more damaged than they were at that time.

The site plan is elongated with what now appears to be two rows of mounds paralleling the shoreline. The regularity of the plan, however, may be artificially produced by the selective removal of mounds during the construction of the modern village. As Voorhies and Gasco (2004:51) admit, "Because of the high degree of destruction, our site map may be only a vague approximation of the appearance of the site at the time of last prehistoric use."

The principal mound at the site is labeled Mound 1 on the site map (Figure 5.4). This was once a tall conical mound some 3 m high in the 1980s (Figure 5.5) but Palmeños report that it had been higher. It has now completely disappeared. A rectangular-shaped plaza occurs on the east and west side of Mound 1. This central area of the site thus appears to have a planned layout, although, as we mentioned above, the grid pattern of the modern village may influence this impression. There is no ball court in the vicinity of Mound 1, where it would be expected. Voorhies and Gasco (2004:51) speculate that two mounds at the western end of the site might have been a ball court, but this is far from certain.

We excavated two test pits in La Palma into well-stratified deposits (Voorhies and Gasco 2004:51-53). We found that the site was occupied from the Late Preclassic though the Classic periods and again in the Late Postclassic period. The most substantial occupation was during the Late Postclassic period, judging from the dense quantities of artifacts that we excavated and that are seen eroding from the bank of the canal.

Las Morenas (MAP-5)

Las Morenas is located southwest of Mapastepec on the eastern bank of the lower San Nicolás River, near its confluence with the inland waterway system that runs parallel to

Figure 5.5.   Photograph of remains of tall, conical Mound 1, La Palma.

the coastline. The site location is an inactive barrier beach. The site is elongated (Figure 5.6), with the long axis parallel to the shoreline. We mapped 47 mounds within an area of 15 ha. A tall conical mound (Mound 27) is positioned near the site center, with a second tall mound east of it. Between these two mounds is a rectangular-shaped plaza. Two pairs of mounds occur within this open space. Another open space lies on the west side of Mound 27, but it is not clearly bounded to form a space with rectilinear sides. There is no ball court at the site.

Hector Neff excavated the site and his findings are described in Voorhies and Gasco (2004:53-58). The site was occupied from the Late Preclassic through the Late Classic periods and then again in the Late Postclassic period.

Coquito (CAP-21); Coquito #2 (CAP-22)

The location known as Coquito lies on a large, inactive beach ridge forming an island southwest of La Palma. This island is within the mangrove formation at the edge of the inland canal that parallels the coastline.

Accordingly, the history of the occupation of the archaeological sites may be tied to the use of this waterway as an ancient transportation route. Carlos Navarrete (NWAF map archives) was the first archaeologist to report this site, although he called it Islona.

We mapped the archaeological zone in two sections, and each was given a separate designation (Coquito and Coquito 2). This procedure was necessitated by the fact that at the time of the mapping, the area between the two clusters of large platform mounds was densely overgrown. Although visibility was very poor within this intervening area, the field crew saw no evidence of prehistoric occupation, so we were unsure whether one or two sites were actually present. When the surface sherds collected from the two areas were analyzed, we found that the two sites were largely contemporaneous, although CAP-22 may have been occupied first, and the Late Postclassic period occupation may have been more intense at CAP-22, than at CAP-21.

CAP-21, the eastern cluster of platform mounds, consists of two large oblong mounds,

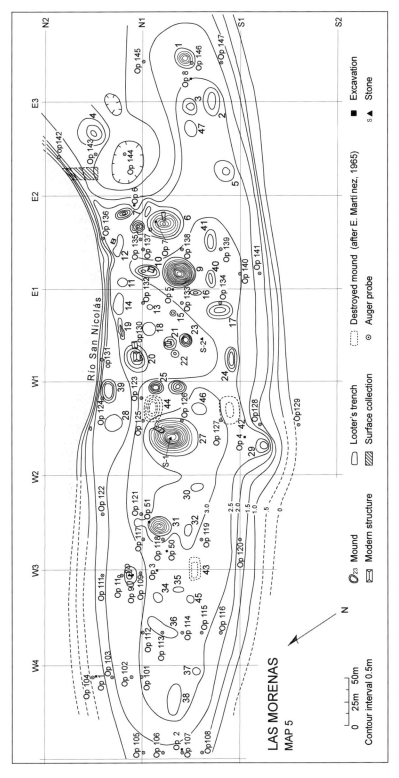

Figure 5.6. Topographic map of Las Morenas (mapped by J.Gasco, B. Voorhies, and H. Neff; drafted by D. Reeves).

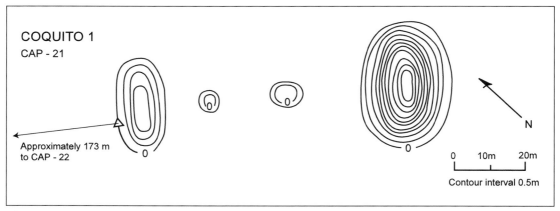

Figure 5.7.   Topographic map of Coquito 1 (mapped by J. Gasco, H. Neff, and B. Voorhies; drafted by A. Nethery).

the highest of which is 5.0 m above the adjacent ground level (Figure 5.7). The long axes of both of these mounds are northeast-southwest so they are oriented at right angles to the strandline of the canal. Between the two large mounds are two small, approximately circular mounds that are less than 0.5 m high. The approximate area of this site is 0.69 ha. It was occupied from the Early Classic through the Late Classic periods, with a less intense occupation in the Late Postclassic period.

CAP-22, is the larger of the two mapped areas. It is 8.41 ha and has 28 mapped mounds, the highest of which is 4.0 m above the level ground (Figure 5.8). The overall site plan is elongated. Mounds are generally oblong in shape and they form several distinct rectangular plaza groups. A second tall mound is located east of the central mound on the opposite side of one of these plazas. There is no ball court. This site has a major occupation spanning the Protoclassic through Late Classic period. After an apparent, but perhaps not real, hiatus in the Early Postclassic period it was reoccupied in the Late Postclassic period. The site is described in Voorhies and Gasco (2004:58-60).

Loma Bonita (CAP-31)

This site was occupied from the Late Preclassic through the Late Classic periods and again in the Late Postclassic period. According to our analysis of surface sherds the occupations

were equally intense throughout. Because the site plan appears typical of that of the Late Classic period we included its description in Chapter 4.

Lomas de Piedra (CAP-11)

This site was occupied during the Classic and Late Postclassic time periods with what seems to be equal intensity based upon the analysis of recovered potsherds from the site surface. We described this site in Chapter 4 where we treated it as anomalous.

Lomas Juana (CAP-35)

Lomas Juana is situated southeast of Acapetahua on an elongated ridge adjacent to and parallel with the ridge on which the Acapetahua site is situated. The site covers an area of approximately 10.67 ha, and we mapped 20 mounds, the highest of which is 2 m (Figure 5.9). This site plan is unlike that of the sites we have described previously.

One striking difference is that there is no centrally located tall, conical mound dominating the site plan. The tallest mound has a small footprint and is only 2 m high. It is located between two oblong, low mounds and is not flanked by rectangular plazas as at the other sites we have described above. Other mounds at the site trend either NW-SE or NE-SW and are perpendicular to each other. Despite this, the layout appears more random than formally

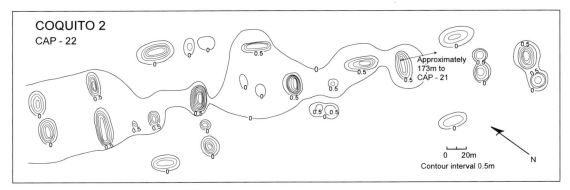

Figure 5.8.   Topographic map of Coquito 2 (mapped by J. Gasco and B. Voorhies; drafted by A. Nethery).

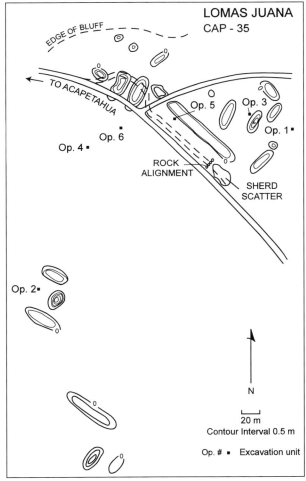

Figure 5.9.   Topographic map of Lomas Juana (mapped with compass, tape, and level by J. Mallory).

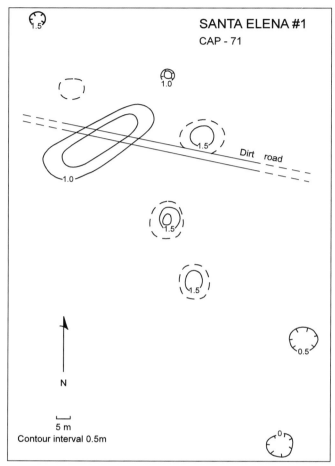

Figure 5.10.   Topographic map of Santa Elena. (mapped by
M. Jaffe; drafted by A. Nethery).

planned. A ball court is located at the top of the hill near an exceptionally long mound. This site may have suffered a lot of surface damage due to modern agricultural activities.

We excavated six test pits at the site. Cultural material was noticeably scant. Further description may be found in Voorhies and Gasco (2004:49-51). Overall, this site is puzzling in several ways, including its close proximity to Acapetahua and the presence of a ballcourt indicating public activities but without the usual other architectural markers found elsewhere. We think this may be a special purpose site associated with the dominant center of Acapetahua.

Santa Elena #1 (CAP-71)

Santa Elena #1 is located at the west entrance to the town of Santa Elena, just southwest of the crossroads to Las Lomitas. Here, the coastal plain is flat and there are no nearby topographic features. The site has five platform mounds in an area of 0.97 ha (Figure 5.10). No regular pattern is evident from the mound layout. From its appearance the site may have been a household cluster. Whatever the case, it consists only of small mounds that are not significantly different from each other.

This site was occupied from the Late Preclassic through the Late Classic and again in the Late Postclassic period. The last occupation appears to have been the most intense, judging from the relative quantity of potsherds from the surface pertaining to each of these time periods.

Loma Eduardo (CAP-52)

This single mound site was occupied during the Late Classic as well as during the Late Postclassic period. Since the intensity of the occupation was judged to be equal for these two periods we have described the site in Chapter 4.

INTRASITE SETTLEMENT PATTERNS AND BURIAL PATTERNS

The group of sites ending in the Late Postclassic period range greatly in size, similar to what we observed in our inventory of sites ending in the Early Classic and Late Classic periods. Nonetheless, very few of the Late Postclassic period sites consist of only one or several small low mounds that we could tentatively interpret as house platforms for isolated family groups. Loma Eduardo might be considered one such example, but because it is a multicomponent site it may have been formed entirely prior to the Late Postclassic period. Normally, we would expect many more small sites than large sites (see Chapter 6), but this is clearly not the case in our site inventory for the Late Postclassic period. One explanation for this finding might be that in Late Postclassic times the inhabitants of our study area lived in densely populated centers where they congregated for their own protection. Another explanation is that isolated rural house sites have become invisible archaeologically because of the practice during the Late Postclassic period of building houses directly on the ground instead of constructing raised platforms. Our data from Acapetahua show unambiguously that Late Postclassic period house locations may have extremely low archaeological signatures, which means that these locations will be easily missed. Therefore, we are unable to address the question with our present data of whether the people of the Soconusco congregated into settlements or were more uniformly dispersed over the landscape (see discussion in Voorhies and Gasco 2004:12-13).

In the larger sites with public architecture such as tall conical mounds, open plazas and ball courts, we see an architectural pattern that we have described previously (Voorhies and Gasco 2004:74ff). This pattern became evident to us when we examined the maps of sites reported here along with other Late Postclassic period sites of the Chiapas coast. The pattern consists of a central tall conical mound with rectangular plazas on its west and east sides. Some of these plazas have plain stone monuments, and others have low platform mounds that may be the remains of altars, as known at other well-studied sites in Meosamerica. Overall, the layout of the Late Postclassic period sites is more formally organized and has more built-in restricted access to open spaces compared with the Classic period sites. Also, the prevalence of ball courts at medium-sized Late Classic period sites gave way to courts being built only at the principal centers in the settlement hierarchy. These ideas are developed more fully in Voorhies and Gasco (2004:75).

What we infer from these intrasite settlement data is that the society in Late Postclassic times became more highly structured and integrated compared with its organization during the Classic period.

Finally, we examine the burial data pertaining to the Late Postclassic period in search of clues about the society during this time period. Four burials, all from Las Morenas, date to the Late Postclassic period (Appendix A: Human Remains). Despite the small sample it is possible to draw some interpretations from these burial data. All four burials were placed in simple pit graves and were found in the fill of one of the excavated mounds at the site. The sample population consists of a child, a young adult male, an adult who is probably male, and another adult whose sex is unknown. The two individuals with surviving teeth, the young adult male and the child, have poor dental health. The adult also has linear hypoplasia on his incisors that documents that in his childhood this man suffered some sort of physiological trauma.

There were no other indicators of pathologies on the four sets of skeletal remains.

Despite the fact that these burials all came from the same mound location, only the young adult male wore personal adornments. These are a beautifully worked obsidian labret (#7029; Voorhies and Gasco 2004:Fig. 5.4) and a copper tinkler (#7027; Voorhies and Gasco 2004:Fig. 5.7), both of which are fabricated from exotic materials and must have been rare and valuable imports. The fact that only one of three adults was so adorned suggests to us that the Las Morenas society was socially differentiated. We might even hypothesize that high social rank was achieved rather than ascribed. This is based upon the idea that the men buried together in the same mound may have been members of the same social group, but the elder men lacked comparable adornments to the younger man. Obviously, such speculations are not well confirmed since the burial sample is too small to test this hypothesis.

In summary, our examination of the intrasite settlement patterns and burial patterns for three chronological time periods leads us to propose that, over time, Soconusco society became progressively more structured, as indicated by an increasing tendency toward formal site layout. At the same time there appears to have been a shift toward more social differentiation throughout the time period under consideration. These findings are in no way surprising, but at the same time it is important to emphasize that our data are far from robust. Particularly, we lack the excavation data needed to provide more convincing answers to some of our questions.

In the final chapter we consider the regional settlement data for the time periods for which we have information.

CHAPTER 6

REGIONAL SETTLEMENT PATTERNS

In this final chapter we examine the settlement data from the Proyecto Soconusco study area from a regional rather than intrasite perspective. Our principal objective is to investigate whether these data can be used to make inferences about the ancient sociopolitical systems of the people who constructed the archaeological sites. Archaeologists often assume that an analysis of regional settlement patterns reveals the political structure of past societies. Although this assumption may be correct, a close study of the literature shows that this proposition is often left unquestioned and thus undemonstrated. As a result there is a lack of middle range theory pertaining to this issue, and the conclusions of many settlement pattern studies of archaeological sites are arrived at by intuitive means. In the following section we seek to clarify some of these issues before specifically addressing the data from our project area.

THE ARCHAEOLOGICAL STUDY OF SETTLEMENT PATTERNS

Settlement analyses of both modern and ancient societies encompass a wide range of perspectives, from focuses on the layout of structures within a single site or architectural group (Fletcher 1977), to regional analyses over large spatial areas (Blanton et al. 1993; Earle 1976; Steponaitis 1981). In the preceding chapters we have tried to tease out regularities in the layout of structures at sites dating to specific time periods. This approach has yielded only moderate insights into the ancient sociopolitical organization of the inhabitants of our study area over time. We focus here on the regional perspective of site size and distribution, as a possible means of detecting the sociopolitical organization in the Proyecto Soconusco study area at different points of time in the prehistoric past.

Archaeologists often approach regional settlement studies by constructing a hierarchical ranking of sites based on site size. They do this with the implicit understanding that in complex societies the sociopolitical functions of site residents change as site size increases or decreases. The divisions of sites into separate size classes, however, are often determined arbitrarily, even though the sizes of sites within a single society actually fall along a continuum (e.g., Adams and Jones 1981; Alden 1979; Johnson 1975). In fact, several archaeologists and geographers have previously pointed out that the analyst *always* imposes arbitrary boundaries onto continuous site size distributions (Blanton 1976:253; Bray 1983:171-172; Marshall 1969; Vining 1955) when site hierarchies are created solely on the basis of size.

Another method employed by archaeologists to use settlement data to understand ancient sociopolitical organization is to create site types based on the presence or absence of particular structural forms (De Montmollin 1989; Weigand 1985), or by size and qualitative differences in architecture (Creamer and Haas 1985). Moreover, analysts sometimes draw political boundaries around the largest sites in a regional hierarchy (MacNeish et al. 1972), and/ or postulate ancient trade and exchange routes based on the geographical distribution of sites of different hierarchical levels (Alden 1979; Johnson 1975).

Once an archaeologist has established a hierarchical classification system of site types (i.e., a taxonomy) for a given region, it then becomes incumbent on the analyst to ascribe meaning to the settlement hierarchy, which itself may be an artificial construct. Frequently, archaeologists equate levels in the settlement hierarchy with levels of administrative decision-making (e.g., Creamer and Haas 1985; Peebles and Kus 1977; Voorhies 1989a); that is, they argue that the site hierarchy reflects political organization. Indeed, Earle (1987:289) mentions that "a settlement hierarchy is perhaps the most frequently used indicator of [ancient] chiefdoms," perhaps because of the implied political centrality in hierarchical arrangements.

All the above approaches have flaws. Archaeological and modern geographical studies have clearly shown that populations arrange themselves upon the landscape in aggregates of various sizes, ranging from settlements of a few structures to large urban centers. What is not clear is how to relate the observed settlement patterns to political structures, although Renfrew (1982:3) claims that in non-industrial societies a correlation exists between size and political primacy.

Vincas Steponaitis (1981) used a site catchment analysis to infer the level of centralization present in the Valley of Mexico during the Formative period. Since he determined that many sites had larger and denser populations than apparently were sustainable through their individual catchment areas, Steponaitis postulated that the flow of tribute must account for the observed site distribution. This, he argued, was indicative of political centralization. Steponaitis also found that the levels of the settlement hierarchy and the degree of centralization generally increased through time from the Middle Formative to the Terminal Formative periods in the Valley of Mexico.

Still, it is entirely possible that such regional settlement studies are simply measuring population growth in an area rather than measuring the degree of political centralization as they claim. As we mentioned, Steponaitis (1981) based his analysis on the observation that the size of some sites in the Valley of Mexico exceeded their catchment areas, but this phenomenon is a typical consequence of population growth. In fact, measures of population sizes in the Valley of Mexico for the Formative period (Blanton et al. 1993) can be correlated directly with the enlargement of Steponaitis's settlement hierarchy. This situation may be similar to that discussed by Winifred Creamer and Jonathan Haas (1985)

who constructed settlement hierarchies for the ancient inhabitants of Central Panama and of the Gulf of Nicoya region in Costa Rica. Because the authors' constructed settlement hierarchy for Central Panama had more levels than did their settlement hierarchy for the Nicoya region, they claim that "chiefdoms" developed in Panama whereas "tribes" were the main sociopolitical forms in the Gulf of Nicoya region. It may be shown, however, that Central Panama sustained a larger population than did the Gulf of Nicoya area (see Cooke 1984; Lange 1984). In other words, Creamer and Haas's (1985) inferences about political structure in the two regions may be merely a reflection of differential population size rather than a reflection of sociopolitical organization.

Archaeologists are well aware that population size and the complexity of political organization are correlated (e.g., Sanders and Price 1968). For instance, in a review of the subject, Anabel Ford (1986:11) states "the organizational structure of society is related to both population size and density." She argues that population growth increases competition for resources, which leads to increased political control over the economy. However, Ben Nelson (1995:614) carefully distinguishes between different aspects of sociopolitical complexity and offers evidence that the scale of a site and the political hierarchy can fluctuate independently of one another. Regarding population size, Nelson (1995:600) believes that: "Population size is not a direct manifestation of political power, yet it may reflect the recruitment of subordinates by a powerful individual or group and also has implications for the ability of an elite to engage in warfare and conduct public-works projects." Although the correlation between population size and the scale of sites is observable, population pressure has not been demonstrated to be a causal mechanism for increasing sociopolitical complexity.

Thus far we have argued that some archaeological settlement hierarchies have been produced by creating arbitrary divisions of what is actually a continuous distribution of site sizes. Moreover, it has not been satisfactorily demonstrated that a link occurs between the number of levels in settlement hierarchies and the complexity of political decision-making. Given these considerations, it appears that the hierarchy of archaeological sites within a given area may simply reflect the size of the population in that area. Since the complexity of site hierarchies is frequently used as an indicator of types of political organization (see Earle 1987:289), when employed by archaeologists, the designations of "tribe," "chiefdom," and "state" (Service 1962) actually may be merely crude measures of the magnitude of population. The suspected correlation between population size and political organization may be spurious in that the observed additional levels of a regional settlement hierarchy may simply reflect increasing population size over time. The most basic inference that can be drawn from the addition of another hierarchical level within a particular settlement system is that the range of site sizes has increased. We now address methods of empirically interpreting differences in site size.

Interpreting Rank-Size Curves

Based upon the foregoing discussion we think it more productive to shift the question in regional settlement analysis from how many hierarchical levels can be intuitively justified with site size data to how curves produced by rank-size relationships might be best interpreted. To do this the archaeologist must first arrange the settlements of a study population in order of their size and then assign each a rank in the resultant sequence. The shape of the curves produced by such orders of rank size are interpreted to show different types of settlement systems.

There are two basic distributions produced by settlement data: a primate distribution and a lognormal distribution. Primate cities were first identified by geographer Mark Jefferson (1939) and are defined by a single city that is disproportionately large when compared to the second largest city in the same settlement system. In contrast, more proportional differences in city size form a lognormal distribution (an exponential curve that forms a straight line when the data are logometrically

transformed) and is exemplified by Zipf's (1949) rank-size rule.

Linguist George Zipf (1932) proposed a law designed to account for the type of continuous curve created by relative word frequencies. The frequency of a word is inversely proportional to its rank, meaning that the second most frequent word only appears half as often as the first. The third ranked word appears 1/3 as often as the first. Zipf's law has been applied to many types of data, including the size distribution of modern cities (Zipf 1949) and archaeological settlements (Hodder 1979). Zipf's law as applied to cities and settlements is often called Zipf's rank-size rule and specifies that the size of the nth largest settlement should be 1/n, with 1 being the size of the largest settlement. On normal graph paper the plot of settlements by size and rank will appear as a concave curve; when plotted on logarithmic paper the data appear as a straight line. This is called the rank-size pattern.

It is critical to understand the processes behind the formation of the continuous rank-size curve if any meaning is to be assigned to it. Since the introduction of Zipf's rank-size rule in 1949, economists and geographers have produced a sizeable body of literature seeking to explain it (see Carroll 1982). In anthropology, the rank-size rule has been criticized for being an observation and not a theoretical model (Hodder 1979:118; Smith 1974:171). Ian Hodder (1979) drew on the work of Brian Berry (1961) and Edwin Thomas (1967) to argue that a rank-size continuum of sites may be the natural result of stochastic processes. Hodder considered 12 archaeological datasets of site sizes and found that random stochastic processes could account for the observed distribution in most cases.

Geographer Brian Berry (1961:583) formed a graphic model of the development of city size distributions based on a study of 38 modern population centers. The model illustrates how a dataset dominated by several large primate cities could shift to a continuous distribution of city sizes characteristic of the rank-size rule and a lognormal curve. He argues that when many random forces are in operation, a lognormal distribution is produced by stochastic mechanisms. In contrast, primate cities occur in societies where only a few forces are affecting the city size distribution within a region. Primacy is defined (Berry 1961:573) as when "a stratum of small towns and cities is dominated by one or more very large cities and there are deficiencies in numbers of cities of intermediate sizes." Berry (1961:587) concluded that the degree of primacy in a given region is not related to either the level of economic development or the degree of urbanization. He also cautioned that even within countries containing primate cities, the smaller centers are often distributed lognormally when ranked according to size.

Archaeologists have used Berry's research to interpret patterns in settlement data, but a review of several such works (Crumley 1976; Hodder 1979) shows that the geographic techniques were applied incorrectly. First, it is often not specified that Berry's graphs were plotted on lognormal probability paper, which can lead to incorrect interpretations. Second, archaeological studies tend to oversimplify the characteristics of a primate pattern by equating fewer and simpler forces with early urban societies (Crumley 1976:64; Hodder 1979:121).

Explaining Lognormal Distributions

We began our discussion by pointing out that many settlement hierarchies are created by archaeologists who produce arbitrary divisions in what is actually a continuous distribution of site sizes. Under these circumstances it becomes problematic to extract any meaning from the resultant classes of site sizes. One possible solution to this problem is to not divide the continuous curve into size classes but instead to examine the overall shape of the rank-size curve. Berry (1961) has illustrated the differences between curves produced by site sizes and hypothesized how datasets could change from a primate distribution to rank-size.

It is helpful to consider in detail a dataset that conforms to Zipf's law. Table 6.1 lists a series of 50 numbers that perfectly illustrate Zipf's rank-size rule: each is inversely proportional to the largest number given its rank. What is evident from the example is that there are many more small numbers compared

with large ones. The above example of Zipf's rank-size rule can be graphically illustrated in a number of ways (Figure 6.1a-c): by fitting a curve to the data points (Figure 6.1a), by logometrically transforming the data, which forms a straight line (Figure 6.1b), or by using arbitrary size classes to create a histogram (Figure 6.1c). Archaeologists familiar with settlement data will be familiar with Figure 6.1c. A large number of data points falls within the first few size classes, and subsequently the data points are separated by increasingly large distances along the axis.

Many measurable characteristics in the observable world form this sort of distribution. Ford (1986:84-85) presents two histograms of the number of archaeological residential units from her survey area, each graphed by the number of person-days of labor required for construction. In both graphs, the majority of the data points lie within the first few labor classes; additionally, the larger the sample size, the more points occur along the far right spectrum of the axis. But such a distribution is not confined to the study of archaeological sites. We have already described how Zipf's law was derived from the relative frequency of words used in a text. The number of research papers authored by scientists (Simon 1972), the distribution of incomes (Marshall 1969), and a multitude of other data (Li 2003) have been shown to conform to the same pattern.

The reason that archaeological site size distributions tend to follow Zipf's rank-size rule probably is due to random growth processes. Economist Xavier Gabaix (1999) has convincingly demonstrated that Zipf's law is the natural outcome of stochastic growth processes on cities. If the positive and negative forces affecting the growth of cities are evenly and randomly distributed, then it can be mathematically demonstrated that over time, the resulting distribution of city sizes will follow Zipf's law.

Primate Distributions

Even though rank-size distributions are formed by evenly distributed random processes (Gabaix 1999), distributions with a primate city

Table 6.1. Zipf's rank-size rule illustrated by a list of 50 numbers representing settlement size. The size of each settlement is inversely proportional to its rank. For example, the size of the largest settlement is 500 units. The size of the 50th largest settlement is 500 (the largest settlement) divided by 50 (the rank), which is equal to 10.

Rank	Settlement Size	Rank	Settlement Size	Rank	Settlement Size
1	500	18	27.8	35	14.3
2	250	19	26.3	36	13.9
3	166.7	20	25	37	13.5
4	125	21	23.8	38	13.1
5	100	22	22.7	39	12.8
6	83.3	23	21.7	40	12.5
7	71.4	24	20.8	41	12.2
8	62.5	25	20	42	11.9
9	55.6	26	19.2	43	11.6
10	50	27	18.5	44	11.4
11	45.5	28	17.9	45	11.1
12	41.7	29	17.2	46	10.9
13	38.5	30	16.7	47	10.6
14	35.7	31	16.1	48	10.4
15	33.3	32	15.5	49	10.2
16	31.2	33	15.1	50	10
17	29.4	34	14.7		

appear to depart from this pattern. Thus, it may be useful to distinguish between rank-size and primate distributions. One way to resolve the question of whether a primate city exists is to examine the spacing of data points along the right side of histograms based on site size, as in Figure 6.1c. The distribution in Figure 6.1c is that of rank-size; that is, the data points fall exactly where one would predict from Zipf's law. Primate patterns as observed by Berry (1961) would exhibit much greater spacing between the data points along the right spectrum of the axis.

Geographers have explored possible causes behind the formation of primate cities (Berry 1961; Linsky 1965). We have noted how Berry did not find a relationship between primacy and economic development or urbanization.

Arnold Linsky (1965) has carried out a much more comprehensive analysis of possible causality behind primate distributions. Linsky assumed that primacy is explicable by universal conditions, and he tested six hypotheses designed to evaluate this premise. Although he did not find any universal conditions to be responsible for primacy in his study of 39 modern countries, he identified certain conditions where it becomes more likely. For example, Linsky found that eight out of ten poor countries have high primacy, whereas approximately half of the wealthy ones do and half do not. He also found that large countries (8 of 9), that is, those with 50 or more people per square mile for over 700 miles, tend to have a low degree of primacy. To summarize his results, Linsky (1965:510-511) concluded that

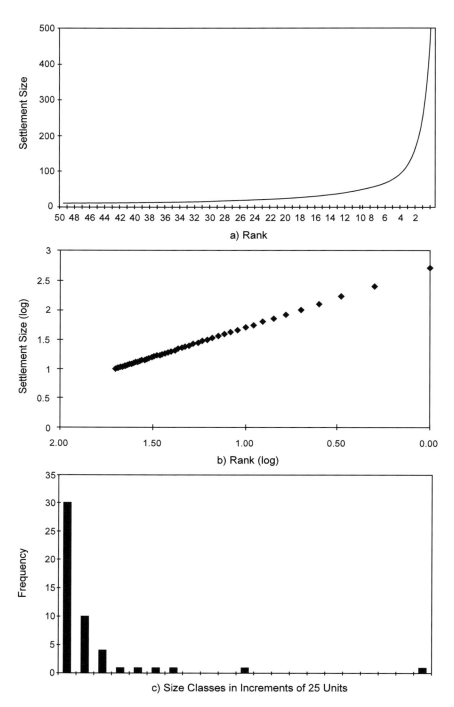

Figure 6.1.   The contents of Table 6.1 displayed in graph form to illustrate Zipf's Rank-Size rule: a) a curve has been fitted to these data (note that the number one ranked site, the largest, is on the right); b) logometric transformation of data produces a straight line; c) data presented in arbitrary size classes typical in archaeological settlement analysis.

small countries are likely to have a high degree of primacy if: the per-capita income is low, the country is highly dependent upon exports, has a colonial history, an agricultural economy, and a fast rate of population growth. Of the countries in the study that were wealthy, economically self-sufficient, had no recent colonial history, non-agricultural economies, and a slow rate of population growth, approximately one-half had a high degree of primacy and one-half did not. In summary, high primacy is not always related to the same identifiable conditions (Linsky 1965:511).

Berry's (1961) suggestion that primate distributions might be created by fewer forces acting upon the system has been interpreted by some archaeologists (Crumley 1976; Hodder 1979) to mean that early states are likely to have primacy in their settlement systems. Linsky's research casts doubt upon this proposition; however, as it is not clear that fewer forces are operating in countries that we know may be prone to primacy. In other words, on the basis of modern studies, differences in political structure or economic development have not been identified as causal factors affecting city-size distribution. Based on Xavier Gabaix's (1999) work, we can state that the difference lies in the distribution of forces that affect city growth. When forces are evenly distributed across the landscape, Zipf's rank-size rule applies. By extension then, primate cities likely result from a concentration of growth forces in one particular city and/or geographic area. Even in primate distributions, the cities ranked below the primate city often follow the rank-size rule (Berry 1961).

Locational Analysis

Fortunately, the problems encountered with the continuous distribution of site sizes in rank-size curves can be avoided if archaeological sites are analyzed in their spatial context (Berry et al. 1962; Marshall 1969). When site sizes are analyzed within their spatial context, functional hierarchies may emerge that are obscured if the region is considered as an abstract whole (Berry and Barnum 1962). As stated by John Marshall (1969:52): "A search for a rank-size

conformation of centres involves abstracting the centres from their real locations, and ranking them by size regardless of their spatial relationships with one another. A search for a hierarchy, on the other hand, requires that the centres be treated literally in situ, that their mutual spatial interrelationships be studied...." If sites are not analyzed with respect to their location, it is inevitable that any resulting hierarchies will simply have been imposed upon the continuum of data by the analyst. Examining the sites in context solves this problem.

Location theory, as articulated by geographers, recognizes the existence of spatial gradients across a landscape. Spatial gradients arise from the recognition that population density and land use increase as one approaches a central place (Morrill and Dormitzer 1979:362). Furthermore, the points highlighted by the gradient surface of a landscape allows for spatial hierarchies to be distinguished.

Central place hierarchies are formed on the basis of the number of functions that a center contains, and not on their relative size. Nonetheless, several studies have correlated modern city size with the number of functions and services being offered within the city (Berry 1967; Berry et al. 1962; Berry and Garrison 1958b; Stafford 1963; Thomas 1960). In a study of small towns in the state of Iowa, Thomas (1960) found that the number of establishments and the number of functional units within a town are directly correlated with the population size. An establishment is defined as a building or office in which one or more functions are performed, and a functional unit is the occurrence of any function (Thomas 1960:11). These definitions become significant when the number of distinct functions is considered because the relationship is non-linear, even though it still increases with population size. That is, the total number of services offered within a city has a direct linear relationship with city size, but the rate at which new functions are added decreases after a given point. These findings were confirmed by later studies (Berry 1967; Berry et al. 1962; Stafford 1963) covering several areas of the United States.

The above findings have resulted from the study of communities embedded in Western economic systems, but the question of how to apply these results to prehistoric societies still persists. In this regard, Berry (1967) has noted that the frequency of periodic markets in non-western societies depends primarily on the surrounding population density. This suggests to us that the number of economic functions performed in a settlement center might still be approximately correlated with population size. Still, the number of economic services offered in a center does not necessarily equate with its place in a political hierarchy. We hypothesize that the amount of labor reflected in the construction effort of public mounds and high-status residences can be used to infer the political rank of a site. We discuss the supporting evidence for this hypothesis below.

Mound Size and Social Status

Archaeologists are comfortable with the assumption that status differences among households can be distinguished by the amount of labor required to construct the respective residences. For instance, Jeanne Arnold and Anabel Ford (1980) used the amount of labor investment in structures at the Maya site of Tikal as a means of determining the status of the former occupants. They (1980:716) state "it is [widely] assumed that upper-class individuals had the power or wealth to manipulate this labor force [of non-elites] for nonpublic ends as well, and that the residential units which these individuals occupied reflected this situation." The article by Ford and Arnold generated substantial discussion (e.g., Folan et al. 1982; Ford and Arnold 1982; Haviland 1982), with most of the voiced criticism resting on the methodological techniques and assumptions specific to the site of Tikal. It is worth noting, however, that not one commentator (Folan et al. 1982; Haviland 1982) questioned the underlying assumption that the status of a household is reflected in the construction of its residence. This premise was simply accepted.

Elliot Abrams (1994:76) also argues from a logical standpoint that the expenditure of labor in residential structures is an accurate indicator of status, and he presents evidence that larger structures provide a "higher biopsychological quality of life" associated with high status compared with smaller structures. In addition to ethnographic studies, Abrams summarizes recent archaeological evidence as demonstrating that "independent glyphic, mortuary, ceramic, [and] architectural studies all conclude that more costly architecture is associated with high levels of social power (Sanders 1989; Webster 1989; Sheely 1991; Hendon 1991; Fash and Stuart 1991; Diamanti 1991)" [Abrams 1994:76-77]. Also, as alluded to by Abrams, it has been successfully argued that status can be determined through the type and number of grave goods accompanying burials (Peebles and Kus 1977).

Mound Size and Political Power

Obviously, being able to equate the size of a residence with the social status of the occupants does not address the issue of political power. Specifically, can the amount of labor investment in public, non-residential mounds be used to infer the political influence of a particular site?

Arnold and Ford (1980:716) point out that Mayanists widely assume the elite segment of Maya society regularly conscripted commoners for public works projects, such as monumental architecture. Ford (1986:14) states that the "presence, frequency, and size of public structures are keys to hierarchical relations among settlements...." She references an article by Steponaitis (1978) that provides two ethnographic cases that substantiate this correlation: the Natchez and the Society Islanders. Steponaitis (1978:421-422) mentions that the administrative center of each Natchez political district contained public and elite structures: "Such a center consisted of a temple and the dwellings of the chiefs and other important personages arranged around a plaza. It was marked by monumental architecture insofar as the temple and/or some of the important dwellings were placed upon pyramidal mounds artificially constructed of earth (Neitzel 1965; Swanton 1911:158, 190-191, 213-214; Thwaites 1900:135)." In regard to the three-tiered political structure of the Society Islanders, Steponaitis (1978:424) summarizes the literature as follows:

Political centers associated with administrative districts at all levels were characterized by the presence of *marae*-structures used in religious ritual. These *marae* were rectangular courtyards, usually paved with stones, and sometimes surrounded by a masonry wall (Oliver 1974:177ff). Within the courtyard were a number of upright stones, and generally a stone platform at one end. *Marae* of many types were built (Emory 1933), but it is quite clear that their size and elaboration were directly tied to the status of the chiefs who used them. Thus, the "tribal" *marae* of a *fenua* (paramount) chief would be a larger and more complex structure than that of the subchief, which in turn would be more elaborate than that of a steward (Oliver 1974:186, 1010, passim). Indeed, such a three-tiered hierarchy of *marae* had been identified archaeologically on Mo'orea (Green et al. 1967:224-225). Other architecturally distinctive features associated with these centers were chiefly dwellings, assembly houses, and/or assembly platforms, all of which are recognizable archaeologically (Green et al. 1967:Table 13; Oliver 1974:170ff).

Thus, it appears that a correlation between the appropriation and display of surplus labor and the loci of political power is real, and this inference can be substantiated through both ethnographic and archaeological evidence.

An additional example reinforces this point. Patrick Kirch (1990:207) has argued "in both Tonga and Hawaii, monumental architecture was utilized by these chiefly elite as symbols through which their dominance was continually asserted." He demonstrates this by combining archaeological information with oral tradition and ethnohistoric information. Throughout his study areas, the largest and most elaborate mounds are found in the central places of the paramount chiefs (Kirch 1990). Monumental architecture requiring less effort to construct appears to correspond with lower divisions in the hierarchical elite administration.

On the basis of these examples, we feel justified in employing measures of the appropriation of surplus labor to identify political centers within the Proyecto Soconusco study area. In many ways, the ability to control labor appears to be a valid definition of political power itself. As Bruce Trigger (1990:127) has stated, "Monumental architecture expresses in a public and enduring manner the ability of an authority to control the material, specialized skills, and labour required to create and maintain such structures." We agree with Abrams's (1994) contention that architecture provides an excellent means by which to study the distribution of political power in ancient society. We now turn to the settlement data from the study area.

ANALYSIS OF PROYECTO SOCONUSCO SETTLEMENT DATA

In this section we analyze the Proyecto Soconsco regional settlement data in order to infer any hierarchical organization that may have been present during the Early Classic, Late Classic, and Late Postclassic periods, the three periods of time in our study for which we are able to address this issue. In our analysis we use site size as a relative indicator of economic function, and we use a labor index to study possible political hierarchies among the sites. The site data are studied in their spatial context for central place patterns and also compared in a temporal dimension as a means of detecting possible changes over time.

Our measure of site size is simply the number of platform mounds recorded for each individual site. We made no distinction between large or small mounds, nor did we distinguish between public mounds and residences. These data for selected archaeological sites in our inventory are shown in Table 6.2.

Our labor index is equivalent to the total volume, reported in cubic meters, of constructed platform mounds for each of the sites. Abrams (1989) urges archaeologists to estimate actual construction effort, expressed in terms of person-days of labor, rather than simply calculating construction volumes, as we have done. However, we are unable to heed Abrams's commendable advice. One reason for this is

Table 6.2. Number of mounds and labor index for Late Classic, Early Classic, and Late Postclassic period sites. The labor index represent the volume in cubic meters of construction fill at each site.

Late Classic			Early Classic			Late Postclassic		
Site	Number of mounds	Labor index	Site	Number of mounds	Labor index	Site	Number of mounds	Labor index
CAC-3	6	53	ESC-6	1	46	CAP-71	6	247
CAP-50	5	156	CAP-28	2	75	CAP-31	28	1741
CAC-8	3	160	ESC-4	3	82	CAP-21	4	1860
CAP-34	4	223	CAP-70	1	125	CAP-35	20	2113
CAP-63	11	272	ESC-7	6	159	CAP-24	22	2570
CAP-66	9	429	ESC-5	2	189	CAP-15	21	2715
CAP-57	2	450	CAP-49	2	223	MAP-5	47	5049
ESC-3	19	476	COM-4	8	365	CAP-22	28	6132
CAP-44	8	504	CAP-48	2	400	CAP-1	55	12638
CAP-58	5	699	CAP-27	2	563	CAP-2	33	?
COM-3	5	754	CAP-62	17	2544			
CAP-45	2	900	ESC-1	14	2816			
CAP-56	6	1340	COM-1	27	3946			
CAP-29	21	1519	CAC-1	30	6378			
CAP-10	3	1557						
CAP-73	25	1592						
CAC-6	19	1760						
MAP-1	15	1985						
CAP-53	19	2341						
CAP-69	2	2700						
ESC-2	89	2973						
MAP-4	38	3101						
CAP-67	7	3102						
CAP-14	14	3311						
CAP-11	58	3355						
CAP-55	34	3708						
CAC-2	25	4124						
CAP-74	19	4321						
CAP-32	35	6465						
COM-6	117	6725						
CAP-9	8	7572						
CAP-75	31	7766						
CAP-5	9	7952						
CAP-1	103	8937						
CAP-30	33	11027						

that we lack the data necessary to determine construction techniques of individual mounds since only a very few mounds were excavated. Therefore, if we were to attempt labor estimates in terms of person-days our only option would be to multiply the construction volume of each site by a constant value. Obviously, such an exercise would not advance our analysis in any significant way.

In order to estimate the volume of constructed platform mounds we use measurements on individual mounds plotted on the site maps. First, the shape of each mound's footprint at a site was subjectively determined to best conform to either a circle or a rectangle. In the case of circular mounds, the diameters were measured on the site maps and converted to meters, whereas the heights in meters were estimated from the contour lines. The volume of each circular mound was calculated using the standard mathematical formula for the volume of a cone (π x radius^2 x height / 3). For mounds with rectangular plans we measured the length and width of each mound and converted the results to meters, whereas we estimated the mound's height in meters from the contour lines. The volume of each rectangular mound was calculated using the standard mathematical formula for the volume of a pyramid (base x height x length / 3). The labor index (i.e., the volume of constructed platforms in cubic meters) for selected sites is shown on Table 6.2.

In order to test the implications of the theoretical discussion in the preceding section, we first plotted the aggregated site data on size and labor values for each time period. In this initial exercise we did not consider the spatial arrangement of the selected sites. Based upon the foregoing discussion we would predict that a continuous exponential curve should be discernible in each case. Figure 6.2a-f illustrates the results of the size and labor ranking of Early Classic, Late Classic, and Late Postclassic period sites. Just as expected, each graph shows a continuous curve characteristic of Zipf's rank-size rule. As discussed above, this pattern may be attributed to stochastic growth processes. The Late Postclassic period data provide the worst fit. This outcome may be attributable to the small sample size (n=9).

If we arrange the same settlement data broken down into arbitrary size classes it corroborates our finding of the low degree of primacy exhibited by site sizes and labor values for each time period (Figure 6.3 a-f). The few sites distributed along the right side of the X-axis in Figure 6.3b are not an indication of settlement primacy but instead are predicted by the rank-size rule; that is, the larger sites are spaced exactly as they should be (cf. Figure 6.1c). Having confirmed our theoretical predictions for aggregate analysis, we will now analyze the sites in their spatial context.

Early Classic Period

Even though the abstracted rank-size curve for the Early Classic period conforms to expectations of the rank-size rule driven by stochastic processes, a central place hierarchy is discernible when the sites are studied in their spatial context. Figure 6.4 graphically represents the relative size of each site as isometric contours based on the number of mounds. A two-tiered central place hierarchy is evident. Three higher order central places are separated by smaller, lower order sites interspersed between the central places. Richard Morrill and Jacqueline Dormitzer (1979) noted that population density increases as a central place is approached, and this is particularly apparent near the site of Tepalcatenco (CAC-1; 30 mounds). Close to Tepalcatenco is the moderate-sized site of Panteón (ESC-1; 14 mounds), and farther out from the central place is the very small site of Lomas Flor (ESC-5; 2 mounds).

The site distribution of the Early Classic period appears to conform to the characteristics of a solar central-place system (Smith 1976b), that is, small sites surround each central place. Carol Smith (1976b:318-319, 338-345) characterizes large-scale arrangements of this type as reflecting an administered economic system that monopolizes a local market upon which the surrounding rural towns are dependent. It is difficult to evaluate this generalization for the Early Classic period since the necessary archaeological knowledge is not yet available. Further complicating our discussion of this period is the fact that the majority of Early Classic sites also had extensive

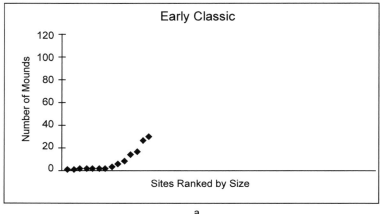

a

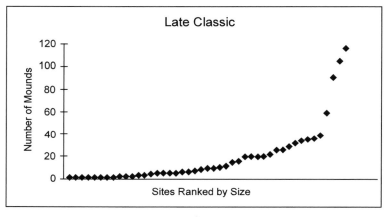

b

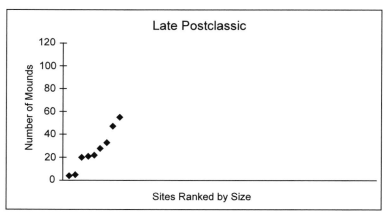

c

Figure 6.2a-c. Proyecto Soconusco sites ranked by size. Sites
abandoned in the (a) Early Classic, (b) Late Classic, and (c) Late
Postclassic are shown on separate graphs.

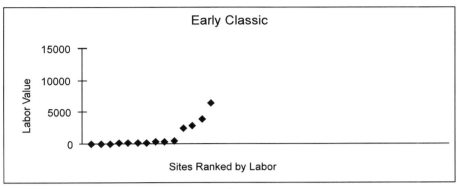

d

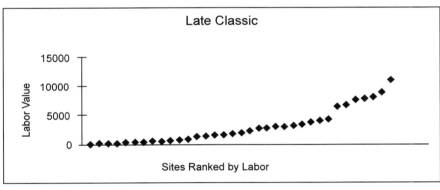

e

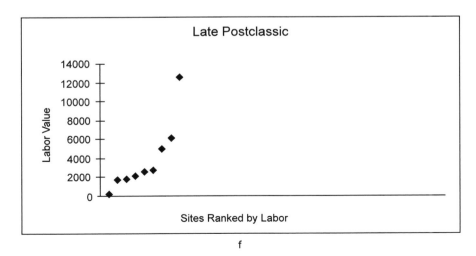

f

Figure 6.2d-f.   Proyecto Soconsuco sites ranked by labor values. Sites abandoned in the (d) Early Classic, (e) Late Classic, and (f) Late Postclassic are shown on separate graphs.

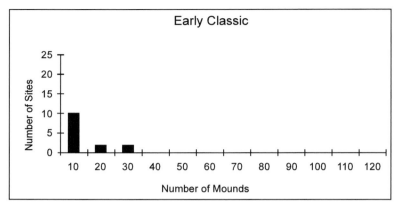

a

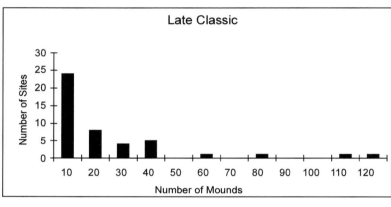

b

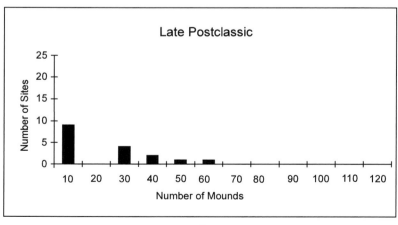

c

Figure 6.3a-c. Proyecto Soconusco sites arranged according to number of mounds. Sites abandoned in the (a) Early Classic, (b) Late Classic, and (c) Late Postclassic are shown on separate graphs.

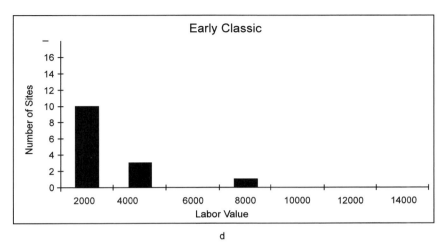

d

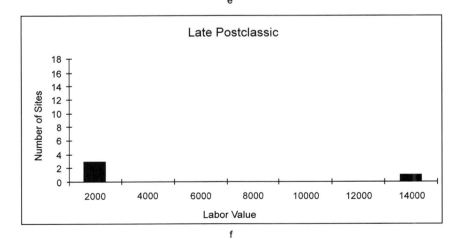

e

f

Figure 6.3d-f. Proyecto Soconusco sites arranged according to labor values. Sites abandoned in the (d) Early Classic, (e) Late Classic, and (f) Late Postclassic are shown on separate graphs.

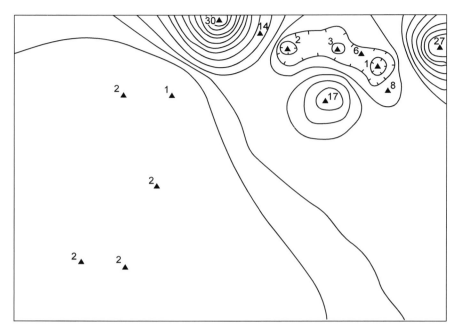

Figure 6.4.   Map of the study area showing the number of mounds at final Early Classic period sites. Isometric lines are drawn based on the number of mounds at each site.

Late Classic components, which substantially modified the present site surface and thus were not included in this analysis.

The distribution of labor values for each site closely correlates with the number of mounds per site ($R^2 = 0.92$). Hence, the topographic landscape representing the number of mounds per site in Figure 6.4 also matches the distribution of labor values. In our analysis, therefore, the economic and political rankings of each site are similar for the Early Classic period.

Late Classic Period

Spatial hierarchies emerge in our analysis for the Late Classic period when locational relationships among sites are considered (Figure 6.5). Three large sites clearly stand out— Acapetahua (CAP-1; 103 mounds), Las Lomas (COM-6; 114 mounds), and Rancho Novillero (ESC-2; 89 mounds). Only a few small sites are located near these large centers. The remainder of the landscape is composed of intermediate sites of approximately the same size, which are

either isolated or surrounded by even smaller sites, typically composed of a few mounds each.

At first it appears that a three-tiered site hierarchy is discernible, composed of the three large sites, numerous intermediate sites, and many small sites. While this is true on a regional scale, it seems likely that only a two-tiered site hierarchy was operational at the local scale because of the spatial distribution of these sites. None of the intermediate-sized sites is located between the three largest centers, and such a pattern does not conform to any of the ideal systems predicted by central place theory (see Smith 1976b:316). Instead, the three large centers are clustered in only one area of the region, whereas the intermediate sized sites are located elsewhere (see Figure 6.5). In essence, then, there are only two levels to the hierarchy: large or intermediate-sized sites dominating nearby smaller sites.

The observation that intermediate-sized sites are not located near the three largest centers may indicate that the area's carrying

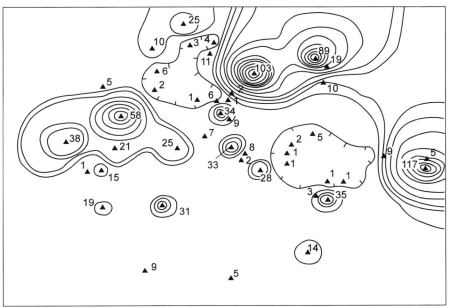

Figure 6.5. Map of the study area showing the number of mounds at final Late Classic period sites. Isometric lines are drawn based on the number of mounds at each site.

capacity was not overcome through tribute extraction. Furthermore, the fact that the three largest centers are clustered and the 11 intermediate centers are also located near one another suggests that, in general, each site was competing economically with a site of similar size and hierarchical level.

An alternative explanation for the observed settlement pattern is that a hierarchical central place system was in existence during the Late Classic period, but that it operated on a scale much larger than that of the Proyecto Soconusco study area. Under this scenario, the three largest centers would be part of a system revolving around a much larger site. At such a scale, a spatial gradient becomes apparent with the intermediate sites blending into the larger centers. Nevertheless, we are not aware of any large Late Classic period sites sufficiently close to the study area to make this scenario a plausible one.

The labor values for Late Classic sites at first appear to suggest that the economic and political landscapes were not congruous in the Late Classic period. The values for site size

assessed by number of mounds and cubic meters of fill (labor) are not well correlated ($R^2 = 0.26$). However, when these data are considered in conjunction with the spatial distribution of sites, a pattern is discernible. The 12 highest labor values tend to coincide with the largest sites (as measured by the number of mounds) in the study area relative to other nearby sites. Figure 6.6 overlays the highest labor values onto the contours produced by the distribution of sites according to number of mounds, as seen in Figure 6.5. Most sites in Figure 6.6 with high labor values are also much larger, in terms of the number of mounds, than the sites immediately surrounding them.

Our analysis thus suggests that the labor and site size values for Late Classic period sites are correlated only when spatial gradients are taken into account. Sites with high labor values do tend to have nearby smaller sites. As we noted for the economic central-place analysis, on the basis of the available survey data, it is possible, but unlikely, that this series of sites was hierarchically organized within a larger regional political system.

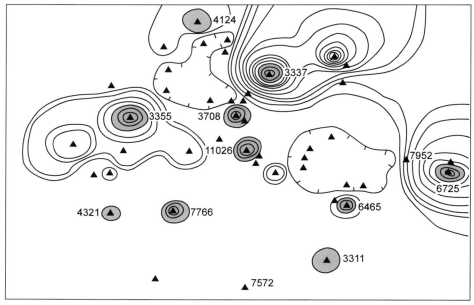

Figure 6.6.   Map of the study area showing the number of mounds at final Late Classic period sites. Isometric lines are drawn based on the number of mounds at each site. Numeric labor values are superimposed upon the map.

Late Postclassic Period

The Late Postclassic period site distribution forms a dendritic central-place system (Figure 6.7). Dendritic settlement systems are capable of encompassing large trade areas and function to funnel goods to one major center (Smith 1976b). Such systems are often found in extractive colonial situations where resources are being removed from the colony for consumption in the colonial homeland. With regard to land-locked dendritic central-place systems, Smith (1976b:319) remarks: "The arrangement is not efficient for interconnecting markets in the agrarian region but is efficient for channeling the upward flow of raw materials from the agrarian region and the downward flow of specialized goods from the major urban center."

The dendritic spatial pattern of Late Postclassic sites in the study area is arranged with the central place near the foothills of the Sierra Madre de Chiapas and the distributaries of the dendritic pattern located in the coastal wetlands (Figure 6.7). The largest Late Postclassic period site, Acapetahua (CAP-1; 55 mounds), and the nearby smaller site of

Lomas Juana (CAP-35; 20 mounds) are situated in the lowest foothills of the Sierra Madre de Chiapas. Approximately halfway between the largest center and the coast is the site of Loma Bonita (CAP-31; 28 mounds). Within the coastal wetlands another similar sized site, La Palma (CAP-2; 33 mounds), is located along a waterway perpendicular to the coast. Finally, several Late Postclassic period sites are situated in a line parallel with the coastline. A natural inland waterway follows the coastline, and three of the Late Postclassic Period sites are located at approximately even distances along it (Voorhies 1989a:123-124; Voorhies and Gasco 2004).

Thus, during the Late Postclassic period the spatial layout of settlements formed a system that allowed local inhabitants to participate in a far-reaching coastal economic network. We hypothesize that several sites were placed at strategic locations in order to facilitate the movement of goods between the dominant central place of Acapetahua-Lomas Juana and the coastal network. Navarrete (1978, 1998) discusses historical documents and ethnographic information indicating that an extensive system

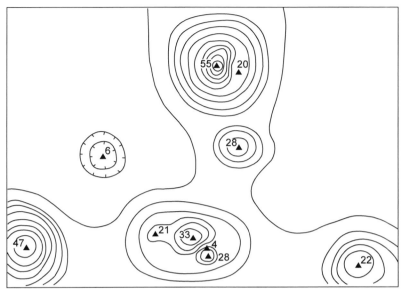

Figure 6.7. Map of the study area showing the number of mounds at final Late Postclassic period sites. Isometric lines are drawn based on the number of mounds at each site.

of canals and natural waterways served as main transport routes in late prehispanic times. Our settlement study corroborates Navarrete's data.

The distribution of labor values for each Late Postclassic period site correlates fairly well with the number of mounds per site ($R^2 = 0.76$). Except for some minor variation, the topographic landscape representing the number of mounds per site in Figure 6.7 also matches the distribution of labor. Acapetahua, the largest site in terms of number of mounds, also has a labor value twice that of the second largest site. Accordingly, the economic and political rankings of each site appear to be similar for the Late Postclassic period settlements.

As we have discussed elsewhere (Gasco and Voorhies 1989; Voorhies and Gasco 2004) there are ethnohistorical sources that shed light on the political organization that occurred during Late Postclassic times on the coast of Chiapas. Evidence from the *Codex Mendoza* and the *Martrícula de Tributos* indicates that eight towns in the Soconusco region were paying tribute to the Aztec empire (Gasco and Voorhies 1989). We are quite certain that the

Acapetahua archaeological site is one of these eight towns, Acapetlatlan (Gasco and Voorhies 1989; Voorhies 1989; Voorhies and Gasco 2004). This substantial Late Postclassic period site is situated immediately adjacent to the modern town of Acapetahua, which has remained in the same location since early colonial times (Voorhies and Gasco 1984). Due to the Aztec practice of conquering only the main towns of provinces (Hassig 1985:101), the importance of Acapetlatlan in the conquest of Soconusco suggests that the site was a paramount administrative center (Voorhies 1989a:98-101), as is indeed suggested by our central place analysis.

Temporal Comparisons

Since our settlement pattern analysis is based on site size and spatial location rather than just site location, we are obliged to use only those sites that were abandoned and not modified by later occupations in our discussion of each individual time period. This procedure has the most serious implications for our analysis of the settlement pattern during Early

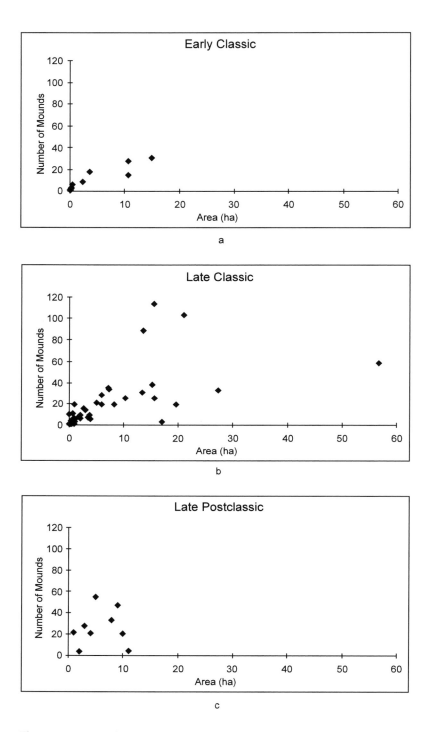

Figure 6.8. Number of mounds per area at sites with final occupations in the Early Classic, Late Classic, and Late Postclassic periods.

Classic period. Even though many sites date to this time period, only a few of them were abandoned at the end of the period and can be used in our analysis. In fact, more sites (n=80) date to the Early Classic period in the Proyecto Soconusco study region than any other period, but most of them were continuously occupied through the Late Classic or even longer. Hence, for the Early Classic, our central place analysis is based on only a small portion of the total Early Classic settlements, most of which are located in one corner of the study area. This situation greatly reduces our confidence in the results of the settlement pattern analysis for the Early Classic period.

The distribution of sites shifted during the Late Classic period compared with the Early Classic period. This is illustrated by the abandoned Early Classic sites in the northeastern portion of the study area (see Figure 6.4). This may be explainable with reference to the Late Classic site distribution. In the Late Classic period, the three largest centers have only a few small sites located nearby. These large centers tended to displace most of the intermediate and small sites, creating immediate hinterlands with very low site densities. The abandonment of the Early Classic sites in these areas may be related to this phenomenon and the growth of dominant Late Classic centers nearby.

The Late Classic period settlement pattern contrasts significantly with that of the Late Postclassic period. A single structured economic or political system is not readily evident from the spatial patterning of sites in Late Classic times. During the Late Postclassic period, however, a highly structured settlement pattern is visible. The dominant central place, Acapetahua, was probably the local political center. The remaining sites are spaced to facilitate the movement of goods to and from the principal center and the hypothesized coastal trade network.

The degree of population aggregation also changed through time. When the number of mounds and the area of sites for the three time periods are used to construct a bivariate plot, population aggregation can be studied.

Reference to Figure 6.8 shows that, on the whole, Late Postclassic sites were more densely populated than most Late Classic or Early Classic period sites. This finding is in agreement with the results of the central-place analysis indicating that the Late Postclassic period settlement was highly structured and formed an administrative economic network.

CONCLUSIONS

Many archaeological settlement pattern studies have only examined a rank-size curve produced from aggregate analysis. Nonetheless, several prior studies have shown that use of this methodology results in a settlement hierarchy created by arbitrary divisions. Geographers have found that the hierarchical structure predicted by central place theory is visible on the landscape if the centers are studied in their spatial context. In archaeology, this type of analysis typically falls under landscape archaeology. Using Bernard Knapp and Wendy Ashmore's (1999) terms, we have focused on the economic and political functions of the constructed landscape rather than on conceptualized or ideational landscapes. Analysis of the Proyecto Soconusco data in this fashion has resulted in the identification of changing central place patterns through time.

During the Early Classic period our data, while plagued with some serious limitations, suggest that the economic and political organization within the study area conforms to a solar central place system. This arrangement is found where competing market centers serve the economic needs of the population in the immediate environs. A highly structured economic system in the Proyecto Soconusco region during the Late Classic period was not evident through the central place patterning. In contrast, the dendritic central-place system of the Late Postclassic period settlement is well-planned and designed to move trade goods to and from the paramount center of Acapetahua. The ethnohistoric sources make it clear that a few decades prior to the arrival of the Spaniards some tribute flowing into Acapetahua was passed along to the Aztecs.

APPENDIX A

HUMAN REMAINS

PROVENIENCE and published source, if any	CLASS	SEX	AGE (years)	TIME PERIOD	GRAVE/SITE LOCATION
Bu 2, Op 5 (MAP- 5) (Voorhies and Gasco 2004:200)	Old adult	F	50+	Protoclassic Period	Pit - Center of site near high, large mound
Pathologies:	Extreme attrition in only tooth recovered; healed lesion from possible scalp infection				
Grave Goods:	None				
Comments:	Skeleton fragmented, no bones articulated. Secondary burial				
Bu 1, Op 7 (CAP-32) (Pfeiffer 1983)	Mature adult	M	40	Early Classic Period	Pit - Periphery of site; between two low mounds
Pathologies:	Teeth completely resorbed; deep indentation in skull along sagittal suture just above lamdoidal suture, possible blow				
Grave Goods:	May have worn shell necklace				
Comments:	Skeleton complete but left leg bones absent. Seated position				
Bu 1, Op 4 (CAP-32) (Pfeiffer 1983)	?	?	?	Early Classic Period	Pit - at mound center near tallest mound
Pathologies:	N/A				
Grave Goods:					
Comments:	No good age or sex indicators. Only bones of lower leg in test pit				
Bu 3, Op 13 (CAP-32) (Pfeiffer 1983)	Young adult	?	?	Early Classic Period	Pit - Near site center, near large low mound
Pathologies:	N/A				
Grave Goods:	None				
Comments:	Only a few bones				

PROVENIENCE and published source, if any	CLASS	SEX	AGE (years)	TIME PERIOD	GRAVE/SITE LOCATION
Bu 2, Op 3 (Com-6)	Infant	?	Infant	Middle Classic Period	Pit - 40 m from site center, between two small low mounds
Pathologies:	N/A				
Grave Goods:	Red ochre, gar pike scales				
Comments:	Reburied (associated w / LC child/young adult(?) also w/ochre				
Bu 1, Op 13 (CAP-32) (Pfeiffer 1983)	Infant	?	Infant	Middle Classic Period	Pit - Near site center, near large low mound
Pathologies:	N/A				
Grave Goods:	Cobble (#372).Also w Bu 2 and 3: 2 obsidian ear plugs (#367); vessel (#358); cobble (#369); 2 jade beads (#366)				
Comments:	Multiple burial. Bones sprinkled w/red hematite; burials encircled w/fine paste sherds. Disarticulated, complete (associated w/ Bu 2 & 3, Op 13)				
Bu 3, Op 10 (CAP-32) (Pfeiffer 1983)	Child	?	10-12	Middle Classic Period	Pit - Periphery of site, near small low mound
Pathologies:	N/A				
Grave Goods:	River cobble (#188)				
Comments:	Primary burial, skull crushed, most bones broken, (associated w/Bu 1&2, Op 10) complete				
Bu 3, OP 12 (CAP-32) (Pfeiffer 1983)	Child	?	5-6	Middle Classic Period	Pit - Periphery of site near no mounds
Pathologies:	N/A				
Grave Goods:	Monzonite bead (#278) placed under bone pile				
Comments:	Skeleton burned, piled beneath skull, Buried w/Bu 2, Op 12 (adult). Hematite (#276)				
Bu 1, Op 10 (CAP-32) (Pfeiffer 1983)	Adult	F?	25?	Middle Classic Period	Pit - Periphery of site, near small low mound
Pathologies:	Teeth-gum infection; lesions at tooth/root junction; abcesses				
Grave Goods:	Shell & red clay (#178)				
Comments:	Primary burial; red hematite around ribs (#179)); arms, ribs, skull, fibulae broken; (associated w/Burials 2&3, Op 10) complete				
Bu 4, Op 10 (CAP-32) (Pfeiffer 1983)	Adult	F?	22-25	Middle Classic Period	Pit - Periphery of site, near small low mound
Pathologies:	Teeth resorbed, much attrition, large cavity in LM2				

PROVENIENCE and published source, if any	CLASS	SEX	AGE (years)	TIME PERIOD	GRAVE/SITE LOCATION

| Grave Goods: | Turtle carapace spindle whorl (#200); river cobble (#191) | | | | |
| Comments: | Primary burial; many bones broken, receding forehead, (associated w/Bu 5, Op 10) | | | | |

Bu 5, Op 10 (CAP-32) (Pfeiffer 1983)	Adult	F	30-35	Middle Classic Period	Pit - Periphery of site, near small low mound
Pathologies:	Deep indentation in skull along sagittal suture above lambdoidal suture, possible blow, much tooth attrition, much resorption				
Grave Goods:	Turtle carapace spindle whorl (#197); river cobble (#196); complete vessel (#195; 979); vessel (#192, 982); vessel (#193, 983)				
Comments:	Arm bones, some ribs broken; hands, sacrum missing; primary burial; vessel similar to Op 12, (associated w/Bu 4, Op 10)				

Bu 6, Op 10 (CAP-32) (Pfeiffer 1983)	Adult	F	25-30	Middle Classic Period	Pit - Periphery of site, near small low mound
Pathologies:	Slight indentation along sagittal suture above lambdoidal suture that could be natural.				
Grave Goods:	Reconstructed vessel (#202; 980)				
Comments:	Primary burial; many bones broken; vessel similar to #279, Op 12				

Bu 1, Op 2 (COM-6)	Young adult	M	?	Middle Classic Period	Pit - near periphery of site, between two small low mounds
Pathologies:	N/A				
Grave Goods:	None				
Comments:	Seated, flexed				

Bu 2, Op 12 (CAP-32) (Pfeiffer 1983)	Young adult	M?	20-22	Middle Classic Period	Pit - near periphery of site, near no mounds
Pathologies:	Teeth show little wear				
Grave Goods:	3 stacked and smashed delicate unused vessels (#279), same type as Op 10; 2 rocks (#280) on top of vessels; 1 vessel (#281)				
Comments:	Bones broken, skeleton apparently complete; hematite (#274); Buried w/ Bu 3, Op 12				

Bu 2, Op 13 (CAP-32) (Pfeiffer 1983)	Young adult	M	20-25?	Middle Classic Period	Pit - Near site center, near large low mound
Pathologies:	N/A				
Grave Goods:	2 obsidian ear plugs (#367); vessel (#358); cobble (#369); 2 jade beads (#366)				

PROVENIENCE and published source, if any	CLASS	SEX	AGE (years)	TIME PERIOD	GRAVE/SITE LOCATION
Comments:	Skeleton apparently complete but broken; bones sprinkled with red hematite; multiple burials (cf. Bu 1 & 3 CAP-32, Op 13); burials encircled with fine paste sherds				
Bu 3, Op 13 (CAP-32) (Pfeiffer 1983)	Young adult	?	?	Middle Classic Period	Pit - Near center of site, near low, large mound
Pathologies:	N/A				
Grave Goods:	2 obsidian ear plugs (#367); vessel (#358); cobble (#369); 2 jade beads (#366)				
Comments:	Multiple burial (cf. Bu 1 & 2, Op 13, CAP-32); bones sprinkled with red hematite; burials encircled with fine paste sherds				
Bu 2, Op 10 (CAP-32) (Pfeiffer 1983)	Mature adult	M	ca. 40	Middle Classic Period	Pit - near periphery of site, near small low mound
Pathologies:	Teeth resorbed; osteoarthritic lipping on iliac crest				
Grave Goods:	Reconstructed vessel (#1089, 999983; similar to Op 12); river cobble (#191); vessel (#183, 999985); vessel (#184, 999984)				
Comments:	Primary burial; red hematite around skull; many bones broken; (associated w/Bu 1 & 3, Op 10)				
Bu 1, Op 12 (CAP-32) (Pfeiffer 1983)	Infant or fetus	?	Infant	Late Classic Period	Pit - Near site periphery, near no mounds
Pathologies:	N/A				
Grave Goods:	None				
Comments:	Burned, covered w/red hematite (#271)				
Bu 1, Op 3 (COM-6)	Child	?	Child	Late Classic Period	Pit - Near center of site, between 2 small low mounds
Pathologies:	Pre-mortem loss of part left foot				
Grave Goods:	Chunk of ochre on foot				
Comments:	Seated, flexed; (associated [same Op] as MC infant, both with ochre)				
Bu 1, Op 1 (MAP-5)	Mature adult	M	40-50	Late Classic Period	Pit - Near site periphery, near no mounds
Pathologies:	Deformed cranium, occipital flattening; large lesion superior to nuchal area; extensive caries, abscesses; osteoarthritic lipping on cervical vertebrae				
Grave Goods:	Ceramic bowl (#7001) and spindle whorl (#7002)				

PROVENIENCE and published source, if any	CLASS	SEX	AGE (years)	TIME PERIOD	GRAVE/SITE LOCATION
Comments:	Seated, cross legged. Femora and left tibia absent at time of burial; 6 molars and pre-molars w/deep grooves at crown/root junction; skeleton articulated				
Bu 1, Op 6 (CAP-32) (Pfeiffer 1983)	Adult	?	?	Late Classic Period	Burial disturbed; no pit observed. Located in southern periphery of site
Pathologies:	N/A				
Grave Goods:	None				
Comments:	Disarticulated and dispersed bones. Badly decomposed				
Bu 3, Grid N3E3 (CAP-8) Reported in Voorhies 1976:67-68.	Adult	M	40+	Early Postclassic Period	Pit
Pathologies:	Osteoarthritis. Mandible is edentulous.				
Grave Goods:	Small avimorphic Tohil plumbate pot				
Comments:	Flexed, seated and facing north.				
Bu 3, Op 9 (MAP-5) Reported in Voorhies and Gasco (2004:56, 200-201)	Young adult	M	20-40	Late Postclassic Period	Pit - in fill of Mound 33
Pathologies:	Linear hypoplasia on incisors; dental abcesses				
Grave Goods:	Obsidian labret (#7029); copper bell (#7027)				
Comments:	Extremely fragmented cranial and postcranial bones. May have been flexed and seated				
Bu 4, Op. 9 (MAP-5) Reported in Voorhies and Gasco (2004:58, 201)	Child	?	4-6	Late Postclassic Period	Pit - in fill of Mound 33
Pathologies:	Possible intentional cranial deformation; caries				
Grave Goods:	None				
Comments:	Poor dental health for one so young. Extended in dorsal position with head to west.				

PROVENIENCE and published source, if any	CLASS	SEX	AGE (years)	TIME PERIOD	GRAVE/SITE LOCATION
Bu 5, Op 9 (MAP-5) Reported in Voorhies and Gasco (2004:58, 201)	Adult	M?	?	Late Postclassic Period	Pit - in fill of Mound 33
Pathologies:	None				
Grave Goods:	None				
Comments:	Only postcranial fragments available. Possibly a secondary burial.Skull may have been removed before burial.				
Bu 6, Op 9 (MAP-5) Reported in Voorhies and Gasco (2004:58)	Adult	?	?	Late Postclassic Period	Pit -in fill of Mound 33
Pathologies:	N/A				
Grave Goods:	N/A				
Comments:	Only leg bones in excavation. Body was prone in pit grave				
Bu 1, Grid N3E3 (CAP-8) Reported in Voorhies 1976:67-68.	Adult	F	approx 30	Intrusive into mainly Classic deposits. May be Early Postclassic	Pit
Pathologies:	Appears healthy at time of death				
Grave Goods:	None				
Comments:	Disturbed and incomplete. Could be a secondary burial.				
Bu 2, Grid N3E3 (CAP-8) Reported in Voorhies 1976:67-68.	Young adult	F	15-16	Intrusive into mainly Classic deposits. May be Early Postclassic	Pit
Pathologies:	Bilateral criba orbitalia				
Grave Goods:	None				
Comments:	Disturbed and incomplete				

MISCELLANEOUS SITES

There are several sites in our inventory that, for one reason or another, do not fit conveniently into the chronological scheme that we have used to organize this volume. In these cases the sites do not shed light on the way particular groups of people organized themselves on the landscape, either because a site is undated, or, as is more often the case, because the site lacks surface features. Each of these miscellaneous sites is discussed below.

Filapa (CAP-13)

Filapa is one of the few sites in the Proyecto Soconusco inventory that consists of surface artifacts without accompanying surface features. The site is immediately east of the town of Acapetahua on the east bank of the Filapa River. Voorhies found the site in 1978 after the area had been recently plowed. At that time there was abundant material visible on the site surface, but two years later only a few scattered artifacts were seen on the surface, and we would not have recognized this as a site had we not known otherwise. We did not measure the area of the sherd scatter.

We have recovered sherds from the site dating from the Late Preclassic through the Middle Classic periods, but the major occupation was apparently during the Late Postclassic Period. We excavated five test pits in order to get a clearer idea of the subsurface features. James M. Kules excavated Operations 1, 3, and 5, whereas Ann Bennett excavated Operations 2 and 4. All the test pits measured 1.5 by 1.5 m.

Operation 1. Kules placed a test pit near the edge of the bluff that runs along the terrace created by the Filapa River. Ceramic sherds were recovered from throughout the uppermost soil layer that extended to a depth of 0.22 m below the ground surface. Significant erosion had probably taken place as this stratum was not a humus layer but clay. A reddish clay statum

that lacked cultural material underlay the upper stratum. This sterile soil layer continued down to bedrock, which was encountered at 0.40 m.

Operation 2. Bennett placed this test pit on a small narrow ridge just above the Río Filapa where numerous sherds and a piece of groundstone were found on the surface. The uppermost stratum was a brown colored sandy clay that extended to approximately 0.10 m below the surface. It contained numerous sherds, together with a piece of green obsidian and an obsidian core fragment. A second soil layer consisting of a coarse, sandy clay extended from 0.10 to 0.30 m, and contained significantly fewer sherds. A posthole probe was dug from 0.30 m to 0.60 m, exposing a third soil type similar to Soil 2.

Operation 3. Kules placed this test pit east of Operation 2 and farther down the ridge. He found a very small number of sherds in the upper humus layer. The humic topsoil ended at a depth of 0.18 m below the surface, at which point Kules encountered a compact sandy clay. So few artifacts had been found thus far that a posthole probe was dug to 0.56 m. Only one sherd was recovered from the posthole, and the excavation was terminated.

Operation 4. In relation to Operations 1, 2, and 3, the fourth test pit was situated to the west and off the ridge. In the uppermost stratum Bennett found modern materials, such as glass, brick fragments, and a shotgun shell. The upper soil layer was approximately 0.10 m thick and was underlain by a sandy clay layer that was 0.20 m thick, similar to that found in Operation 2. Bennett found that sherds decreased and ended at a depth of 0.40 m. She also recovered a piece of green obsidian in this stratum. Coarse sandy clay was encountered and probed with a posthole to a depth of approximately 0.60 m below the surface.

Operation 5. Bennett placed this test pit west of Operation 1 on level ground. A dense red clay occurred underneath the topsoil at a depth of 0.06 m, and this soil layer was excavated to 0.30 m. Bennett collected nearly 80 sherds and one piece of obsidian from the red clay between 0.06 and 0.20 m, but she found only 20 sherds between 0.20 and 0.30 m. Bennett placed a posthole probe in the center of the unit that reached a depth of 0.75 m. No cultural material was found, and the test pit was backfilled.

Maxtate (CAP-20)

This site is located on an inactive barrier beach just west of La Palma, within the mangrove formation of the littoral zone. The site was first detected by means of photo imagery and verified in the field during the first season of Proyecto Soconusco.

The site consists of three low mounds, which according to local informants were created during salt-making activities that had taken place approximately 50 years earlier. Salt is no longer made in the study area, but some of the older people of La Palma can recall when this was done. The mounds have irregular surfaces as expected for recently formed mounds resulting from the *sal cocida* process (Andrews 1983). Bricks and coarse sherds are eroding out of two of the three mounds. The sherds date to the Late Preclassic through the Late Classic periods. Because of this, the site has been plotted on the chronology chart (Figure 1.5) as having been in use during that span of time. This is possible, of course, but it is also certain that the mounds themselves date to the historic period.

We did not map the site nor determine its area.

San Andrés (CAP-25)

This site is located within the mangrove formation on an inactive beach ridge called Isla San Andrés. The island is close to the mouth of the estuary in its 1964 position, the date of the aerial photographs we used during the reconnaissance.

This site consists of small sandy mounds that contrast sharply with most mounds within the site inventory, which are rich in clay. In addition to being made of sandy soil, rather than the clay usually found in mounds in the wetland environment, the surface contours of the mounds at San Andrés are irregular and do not form the smooth contours seen elsewhere. Immediately, then, the site's appearance suggests a function different from that of most sites. According to local informants, this location was used for making salt in recent times. Evidently, the mounds, rather than being intentional constructions for supporting superstructures, apparently are the result of back dirt accumulating after the soil has been washed in order to remove the salt (i.e., *sal cocida*; Andrews 1983). According to local informants, salt making was abandoned approximately 50 years ago because of the establishment of commercial salt making at Salina Cruz, Oaxaca.

We did not determine either the site area or number of mounds.

Zoológico (CAP-23)

Zoológico is one of the few sherd scatter sites without accompanying mound features that we found in the study area. It is located on an island formed by an inactive beach ridge southwest of Laguna Pansacola and within the mangrove formation. The field crew discovered the site during the reconnaissance field season. It is part of La Encrucijada, a biological reserve managed by the Instituto de Historia Natural del Estado de Chiapas.

The area from which sherds were collected measures some 50 m parallel to the adjacent canal and is approximately 25 m wide. We did not draw a site map since we did not see any surface features. We found sherds dating from the Early through Late Classic periods, but the most intense occupation, as indicated by abundance of sherds, was during the Late Postclassic period.

Palillo (CAP-19)

Palillo is a small sandy island, located north of Laguna Teculapa and east of the Las Garzas

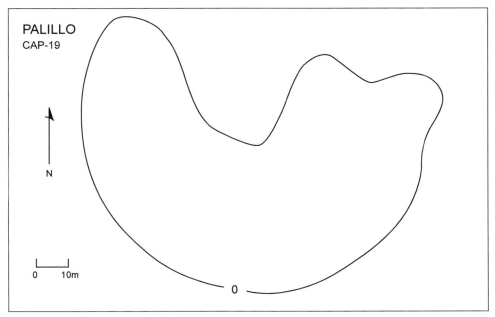

Figure B.1. Topographic map of Palillo (mapped with compass, tape, and level by B. Voorhies).

embaracadero. It is situated within the wetlands where mangrove, madresal, and herbaceous swamp formations are in close proximity. The site itself is surrounded by herbaceous swamp. We first identified the site from photo imagery and subsequently ground verified its presence during the first field season of Proyecto Soconusco.

The island is small (0.68 ha) and low-lying; it is only approximately 0.5 m above the water level (Fig. B.1). The site is not inhabitable on a permanent basis today because of the certainty of flooding during the wet season. The island is flat and has no artificial mound platforms. Because of these considerations we conjecture that the island probably was used as a temporary encampment for fishing and collecting activities but was never occupied on a permanent basis.

On the site surface we found ecofacts that were probably recent, as well as prehistoric lithics and sherds. The sherds date to the Late Preclassic through the Late Classic periods.

Metate (CAC-9)

We found an isolated bedrock metate about 200 m south of the Pan American Highway

(Mex 200) on Transect E17 (Figure 1.16). The metate is located on a hilltop and there are no other nearby prehistoric features such as artifacts or platform mounds. For this reason we do not know the date of this unusual feature. Since the bedrock metate is not associated with other cultural features, we conclude that it is a specialized activity area. We are unable to hazard a guess why the metate was placed in its location but surmise that it was near to resources that required pulverizing.

The metate has been carved into a large granodiorite erratic, so strictly speaking it is not in bedrock. The basin is 57 cm long, 30 cm wide, and has a maximum depth of 11 cm. Voorhies described this feature and illustrated it with a photograph (Voorhies 2004:250)

Delgado (1965:73) reports a bedrock mortar at Santa Rosa near the Isthmus of Tehuantepec but gives no other details. Lee (1969:119) describes a limestone boulder mortar at Izapa with three separate basins. We found no other similar features in the Proyecto Soconusco study area.

In 1991, Douglas Kennett dug a small shovel pit about 1.5 m from the boulder with the metate.

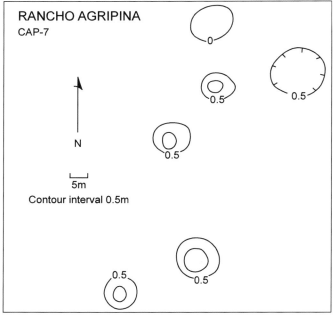

Figure B.2.   Topographic map of Ranch Agripina (sketch map by A. Gerstle, M. Jaffe, and J. Mallory; drafted by A. Nethery).

Most of the recovered sherds were utilitarian wares dating to the Classic period (Voorhies 2004:119-121). In light of the comparative data and the age of the ceramics deposited near the site it cannot be argued convincingly that this is a preceramic site as Voorhies once suspected; however, an early date cannot be discounted which means that the metate's age remains unknown.

Calicante (CAC-5)

This is a historic construction of stone located on the east side of the Jalapa River between the Pan American Highway and the rail line. The feature consists of a retaining wall of mortared river cobbles that parallels the river for approximately 30 m. The wall is 0.5 m high with its base at river level. This wall joins a solid construction that has a passageway opening onto the river and the adjacent hill. The passageway once had wooden lintels that have left their impressions in the mortar. The passageway must be under water when the water is high. We suspect that this feature is the remains of a

mill of some kind. No artifacts were found in association, and we were not able to precisely determine its age other than recognizing that it is historic.

Rancho Agripina (CAC-7)

This small site was discovered during the survey of Transect E17 (Figure 1.16). It is located southwest of Acacoyagua, approximately 1.25 km south of Route 200. This site is situated on top of a ridge. It consists of only five low mounds and a depression that may be a borrow pit (Fig. B.2). This seems to be a small residential site as none of the mounds is large enough to hint of a public function. The site area is 0.37 ha, and the highest mound is 0.5 m.

Although we collected a small bag of sherds from the site surface, none of the sherds was diagnostic and the site remains undated.

Lomas Estubillo (CAP-51)

This site is located on the middle gradient of the coastal plain on the east side of the road leading southwest from Bonanza. Here, the

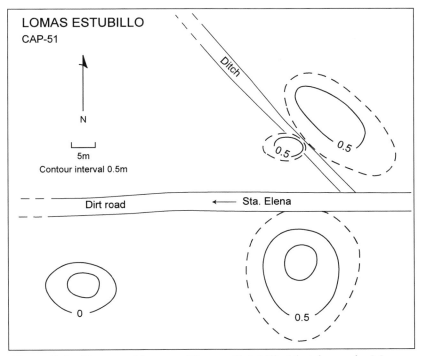

Figure B.3. Topographic map of Lomas Estubillo (sketch map by M. Jaffe; drafted by A. Nethery).

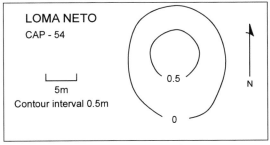

Figure B.4. Topographic map of Loma Neto (sketch map by A. Gerstle, M. Jaffe, and J. Mallory; drafted by A. Nethery).

topography is flat. This site is small, consisting of four mounds in an area of 0.52 ha (Fig. B.3). The highest of these is between 0.5 and 1.0 m. This is probably a residential site judging from the size of the platform mounds.

The field crew did not find any surface artifacts, so this site remains undated.

Loma Neto (CAP-54)

Loma Neto was discovered during the survey of Transect B8 (Figure 1.9). It is located on the west side of the road leading southwest from Bonanza. The topography is flat in the vicinity of the site. Consisting of a single low mound, the site area is 0.02 ha (Fig. B.4). The mound is only a half meter high.

No artifacts were observed on the site surface, so it remains undated.

REFERENCES CITED

ABRAMS, ELLIOT M.
1989 Architecture and Energy: An Evolutionary Perspective. In *Archaeological Method and Theory Vol 1*, edited by M. Schiffer, pp.47-88. University of Arizona Press, Tucson.

1994 *How the Maya Built Their World: Energetics and Ancient Architecture.* University of Texas Press, Austin.

ADAMS, R. E. W. AND RICHARD C. JONES
1981 Spatial Patterns and Regional Growth Among Classic Maya Cities. *American Antiquity* 46:301-322.

ALDEN, JOHN R.
1979 A Reconstruction of Toltec Period Political Units in the Valley of Mexico. In *Transformations: Mathematical Approaches to Culture Change*, edited by Colin Renfrew and Ken. L. Cooke, pp. 169-200. Academic Press, New York.

ANDREWS, ANTHONY P.
1983 *Maya Salt Production and Trade.* University of Arizona Press, Tucson.

ARNOLD, JEANNE E., AND ANABEL FORD
1980 A Statistical Examination of Settlement Patterns at Tikal, Guatemala. *American Antiquity* 45:713-726.

BERRY, BRIAN J. L.
1961 City Size Distributions and Economic Development. *Economic Development and Cultural Change* 9:573-587.

1967 *Geography of Market Centers and Retail Distribution.* Prentice-Hall Inc., Englewood Cliffs.

BERRY, BRIAN J. L., AND H. GARDINER BARNUM
1962 Aggregate Relations and Elemental Components of Central Place Systems. *Journal of Regional Science* 4:35-68.

BERRY, BRIAN J. L., H. GARDINER BARNUM, AND ROBERT J. TENNANT
1962 Retail Location and Consumer Behavior. *Regional Science Association, Papers and Proceedings* 9:65-106.

BERRY, BRIAN J. L., AND WILLIAM L. GARRISON
1958a Recent Developments of Central Place Theory. *Regional Science Association, Papers and Proceedings* 4:107-120.

1958b The Functional Bases of the Central Place Hierarchy. *Economic Geography* 34:145-154.

BLANTON, RICHARD E.
1976 Anthropological Studies of Cities. *Annual Review of Anthropology* 5:249-264.

BLANTON, RICHARD E., STEPHEN A. KOWALEWSKI, GARY FEINMAN, AND JILL APPEL
1993 Ancient Mesoamerica: *A Comparison of Change in Three Regions.* Cambridge University Press, New York.

BRAY, WARWICK
1983 Landscape with Figures: Settlement Patterns, Locational Models, and Politics in Mesoamerica. In *Prehistoric Settlement Patterns: Essays in Honor of Gordon R. Willey,* edited by Evon Z. Vogt and Richard. M. Leventhal, pp. 167-193. University of New Mexico Press and Peabody Museum of Archaeology and Ethnology, Cambridge.

CARROLL, G.
1982   National City-Size Distribution: What do we Know after 67 Years of Research? *Progress in Human Geography, 6:1-43.*

CHAPMAN, GRAHAM P.
1970   The Application of Information Theory to the Analysis of Population Distributions in Space. *Economic Geography* 46:317-31.

COOKE, RICHARD
1984   Archaeological Research in Central and Eastern Panama: A Review of Some Problems. *In The Archaeology of Lower Central America,* edited by Frederick W. Lange and Doris. Z. Stone, pp. 263-302. University of New Mexico Press, Albuquerque.

CREAMER, WINIFRED AND JONATHON HAAS
1985   Tribes Versus Chiefdoms in Lower Central America. *American Antiquity* 50:738-754.

CRUMLEY, CAROLE L.
1976   Toward a Locational Definition of State Systems of Settlement. *American Anthropologist* 78:59-73.

CULEBRO, C. ALBERTO
1939   Chiapas prehistórico: Su arqueología. Folleto No. 1. Huixtla, Chiapas, Mexico.

DE MONTMOLLIN, OLIVER
1989   *Settlement Survey in the Rosario Valley, Chiapas,Mexico.* Papers of the New World Archaeological Foundation No. 57. Brigham Young University, Provo.

DIAMANTI, M.
1991   *Domestic Organization at Copan: Reconstruction of Elite Maya Households through Ethnographic Models.* Unpublished Ph.D.

dissertation, Department of Anthropology, Pennsylvania State University, University Park.

DELGADO, AUGUSTÍN
1965   *Excavations at Santa Rosa, Chiapas, Mexico.* Papers of the New World Archaeological Foundation, No. 17, Brigham Young University, Provo.

DRUCKER, PHILIP
1947   Field notebook entitled "Survey (of) Gulf of Tehuantepec Coast, N.G.S.--Smithsonian Institution Expedition, February to June, 1947". The National Anthropological Archives, Smithsonian Institution.

1948   Preliminary Notes on an Archaeological Survey of the Chiapas Coast. *Middle American Research Records* 1:151-169.

EARLE, TIMOTHY K.
1976   A Nearest-Neighbor Analysis of Two Formative Settlement Systems. In *The Early Mesoamerican Village,* edited by Kent V. Flannery, pp. 196-223. Academic Press, New York.

1987   Chiefdoms in Archaeological and Ethnohistorical Perspective. *Annual Review of Anthropology* 16:279-308.

Emory, Kenneth P.
1933   Stone Remains in the Society Islands. *Bernice P. Bishop Museum Bulletin,* No. 116. Honolulu.

FASH, WILLIAM AND DAVID STUART
1991   Dynastic History and Cultural Evolution at Copan, Honduras. In *Classic Maya Political History,* edited by T. Patrick Culbert, pp. 147-179. Cambridge University Press, Cambridge.

FLETCHER, ROLAND
1977   Settlement Studies. In *Spatial
        Archaeology,* edited by David L.
        Clarke, pp. 47-162. Academic Press,
        Orlando.

FOLAN, WILLIAM J., ELLEN R. KINTZ, LORAINE A.
FLETCHER, AND BURMA H. HYDE
1982   An Examination of Settlement Patterns
        at Coba, Quintana Roo, Mexico,
        and Tikal, Guatemala: A Reply to
        Arnold and Ford. *American Antiquity*
        47:430-435.

FORD, ANABEL
1986   *Population Growth and Social
        Complexity: An Examination
        of Settlement and Environment
        in the Central Maya Lowlands.*
        Anthropological Research Papers No.
        35. Arizona State University, Tempe.

FORD, ANABEL, AND JEANNE E. ARNOLD
1982   A Reexamination of Labor Investments
        at Tikal: Reply to Haviland, and Folan,
        Kintz, Fletcher, and Hyde. *American
        Antiquity* 47:436-440.

GABAIX, XAVIER
1999   Zipf's Law for Cities: An Explanation.
        The Quarterly Journal of Economics
        114:739-767.

GARCÍA-DES LAURIERS, CLAUDIA
2007   *Proyecto Arqueológico Los Horcones:
        Investigating the Teotihuacan Presence
        of the Pacific Coast of Chiapas,
        Mexico.* Unpublished dissertation,
        Department of Anthropology,
        University of California, Riverside.

GASCO, JANINE AND BARBARA VOORHIES
1989   The Ultimate Tribute: The Role of
        the Soconusco as an Aztec Tributary.
        In *Ancient Trade and Tribute:
        Economies of the Soconusco Region
        of Mesoamerica,* edited by Barbara
        Voorhies, pp. 48-94. University of Utah
        Press, Salt Lake City.

GREEN, ROGER C., KAYE GREEN, ROY A.
RAPPAPORT, ANN RAPPAPORT, AND JANET M.
DAVIDSON
1967   Archaeology on the Island of Mo'orea,
        French Polynesia. *Anthropological
        Papers of the American Museum of
        Natural History* 51, Part 2. New York.

HASSIG, ROSS
1985   *Trade, Tribute, and Transportation:
        The Sixteenth-Century Political
        Economy of the Valley of Mexico.*
        University of Oklahoma Press,
        Norman.

HAVILAND, WILLIAM A.
1982   Where the Rich Folks Lived: Deranging
        Factors in the Statistical Analysis of
        Tikal Settlement. *American Antiquity*
        47:427-429.

HENDON, JULIA A.
1991   Status and Power in Classic Maya
        Society: An Archaeological Study.
        American Anthropologist 93:894-918.

HODDER, IAN
1979   Simulating the Growth of Hierarchies.
        In *Transformations: Mathematical
        Approaches to Culture Change,* edited
        by Colin Renfrew and Kenneth L.
        Cooke, pp. 117-144. Academic Press,
        New York.

JEFFERSON, MARK
1939   The Law of the Primate City.
        Geographical Review 29:226-232.

JOHNSON, GREGORY A.
1972   A Test of the Utility of Central Place
        Theory in Archaeology. In *Man,
        Settlement, and Urbanism*, edited by
        Peter J. Ucko, Ruth Tringham, and
        Geoffery W. Dimbleby, pp. 769-785.
        Gerald Duckworth, London.

1975   Locational Analysis and the
        Investigation of Uruk Local Exchange
        Systems. In *Ancient Civilization and*

Trade, edited by Jeremy A. Sabloff and C. C. Lamberg-Karlovsky, pp. 285-339. A School of American Research Book. University of New Mexico Press, Albuquerque.

KENNETT, DOUGLAS J. AND BARBARA VOORHIES
2001   *Informe de campo: Proyecto costero arcaico-formativo, Chiapas.* Submitted to the Instituto Nacional de Antropología e Historia, Mexico.

KENNETT, DOUGLAS J., BARBARA VOORHIES AND SARAH B. MCCLURE
2002   Cerritos: An Early Fishing-Farming Community on the Pacific Coast of Mexico. *Antiquity* 76:631-632.

KENNETT, DOUGLAS J., BARBARA VOORHIES, JOHN G. JONES, HECTOR NEFF, DOLORES R. PIPERNO, THOMAS A. WAKE, KARRY L. BLAKE, BRENDAN CULLETON, JOSUÉ AUGUSTO GÓMEZ GARCÍA, AND NATALIA MARTÍNEZ TAQUEÑA
2007   *Informe tecnico final de Proyecto Arcaico-Formativo: Costa de Chiapas (Temporada 2005).* Submitted to the Instituto Nacional de Antropología e Historia, Mexico.

KING, LESLIE J.
1984   *Central Place Theory.* Scientific Geography Series, Volume 1. Grant I. Thrall, Series Editor. Sage Publications, Beverly Hills.

KIRCH, PATRICK V.
1990   Monumental Architecture and Power in Polynesian Chiefdoms: a Comparison of Tonga and Hawaii. *World Archaeology* 22(2):206-222.

KNAPP, A. BERNARD AND WENDY ASHMORE
1999   Archaeological Landscapes: Constructed, Conceptualized, Ideational. In *Archaeologies of Landscape: Contemporary Perspectives,* edited by Wendy Ashmore and A. Bernard Knapp, pp. 1-30. Blackwell Publishers, Oxford.

LANGE, FREDERICK W.
1984   Archaeological Research in Central and Eastern Panama: A Review of Some Problems. In *The Archaeology of Lower Central America*, edited by Frederick W. Lange and Doris Z. Stone, pp. 263-302. University of New Mexico Press, Albuquerque.

LINSKY, ARNOLD S.
1965   Some Generalizations Concerning Primate Cities. *Annals of the Association of American Geographers* 55:506-513.

LI, WENTIAN
2003   Zipf's Law Everywhere. *Glottometrics* 5:14-21.

LORENZO, JOSÉ LUIS
1955   Los concheros de la costa de Chiapas. *Anales del Instituto Nacional de Antropología e Historia* 7:41-50. México.

MACNEISH, RICHARD S., FREDERICK A. PETERSON, AND JAMES A. NEELY
1972   The Archaeological Reconnaissance. In *The Prehistory of the Tehuacán Valley, Vol. 5: Excavations and Reconnaissance*, edited by Richard S. MacNeish, M. L. Fowler, A. García Cook, F. A. Peterson, A. Nelken-Turner, and J. A. Neely, pp. 341-495. University of Texas Press, Austin.

MARSHALL, JOHN U.
1969   *The Location of Service Towns: An Approach to the Analysis of Central Place Systems.* University of Toronto Press, Toronto.

MORRILL, RICHARD L., AND JACQUELINE M. DORMITZER
1979   *The Spatial Order: An Introduction to Modern Geography.* Duxbury Press, North Scituate.

NAVARRETE, CARLOS
1978   The Prehispanic System of Communications Between Chiapas and Tabasco. In *Mesoamerican Communication Routes and Cultural Contacts*, edited by Thomas A. Lee, Jr., and Carlos Navarrete, pp. 75-106. Papers of the New World Archaeological Foundation, No. 40. Brigham Young University, Provo.

1998   La navegación en la costa de Chiapas. *Arqueología* 6 (33):32-39.

n.d.   Resúmen de las exploraciones del reconocimiento arqueólogico de la costa de Chiapas (region del Soconusco) en la temporada de 1969. Manuscript in the archives of the New World Archaeological Foundation, San Cristobal de las Casas, Chiapas, Mexico.

NEFF, HECTOR
1984   *The Developmental History of the Plumbate Pottery Industry in the Eastern Soconusco Region, A.D. 600 through A.D. 1250.* Unpublished Ph.D. dissertation, Department of Anthropology, University of California, Santa Barbara.

NEITZEL, ROBERT S.
1965   Archaeology of the Fatherland Site: The Grand Village of the Natchez. *Anthropological Papers of the American Museum of Natural History* 51, Part 1.

NELSON, BEN A.
1995   Complexity, Hierarchy, and Scale: A Controlled Comparison Between Chaco Canyon, New Mexico, and La Quemada, Zacatecas. *American Antiquity* 60:597-618.

OLIVER, DOUGLAS L.
1974   *Ancient Tahitian Society.* University Press of Hawaii, Honolulu.

PEEBLES, CHRISTOPHER S. AND SUSAN M. KUS
1977   Some Archaeological Correlates of Ranked Societies. *American Antiquity* 42:421-448.

PFEIFFER, LINDA
1983   *Pottery Production and Extralocal Relations at Rio Arriba, Chiapas, Mexico.* Unpublished Ph.D. dissertation, Department of Anthropology, University of California, Santa Barbara.

1989   The Evidence for Pottery Production at Rio Arriba. In *Ancient Trade and Tribute: Economies of the Soconusco Region of Mesoamerica,* edited by Barbara Voorhies, pp. 157-174. University of Utah Press, Salt Lake City.

PIÑA CHAN, ROMAN
1967   *Atlas aqueológico de la Republica Mexicana: Chiapas.* Instituto Nacional de Antropología e Historia, México.

RENFREW, COLIN
1982   Socio-economic Change in Ranked Societies. In *Ranking, Resource and Exchange,* edited by Colin Renfrew and Steven Shennan, pp. 1-8. Cambridge University Press, Cambridge.

SANDERS, WILLIAM T.
1989   Household, Lineage and the State in 8th-Century Copan. In *House of the Bacabs, Copan: A Study of the Iconography, Epigraphy and Social Context of a Maya Elite Structure,* edited by David Webster, pp. 89-105. Dumbarton Oaks, Washington, D.C.

SANDERS, WILLIAM T., AND BARBARA J. PRICE
1968   *Mesoamerica: The Evolution of a Civilization.* Random House, New York.

SERVICE, ELMAN. R.
1962   *Primitive Social Organization.* Random House, New York.

SHEELY, J.
1991 Structure and Change in a Late Classic Maya Domestic Group at Copan, Honduras. *Ancient Mesoamerica* 2(1):1-19.

SIMON, HERBERT A.
1972 The Sizes of Things. In *Statistics: A Guide to the Unknown,* edited by Judith M. Tanur, pp. 195-202. Holden-Day, Inc., San Francisco.

SMITH, CAROL A.
1974 Economics of Marketing Systems: Models from Economic Geography. *Annual Review of Anthropology* 3:167-201.

1976a Regional Economic Systems: Linking Geographical Models and Socioeconomic Problems. In *Regional Analysis, Volume 1: Economic Systems,* edited by Carol A. Smith, pp. 3-67. Academic Press, New York.

1976b Exchange Systems and the Spatial Distribution of Elites: The Organization of Stratification in Agrarian Societies. In *Regional Analysis, Volume 2: Social Systems*, edited by Carol A. Smith, pp. 309-374. Academic Press, New York.

STAFFORD, HOWARD A.
1963 The Functional Bases of Small Towns. *Economic Geography* 39:165-175.

STEPONAITIS, VINCAS P.
1978 Location Theory and Complex Chiefdoms: A Mississippian Example. In *Mississippian Settlement Patterns,* edited by Bruce D. Smith, pp. 417-453. Academic Press, New York.

1981 Settlement Hierarchies and Political Complexity in Nonmarket Societies: The Formative Period of the Valley of Mexico. *American Anthropologist* 83:320-363.

SWANTON, JOHN R.
1911 Indian Tribes of the Lower Mississippi Valley and Adjacent Coast of the Gulf of Mexico. *Bureau of American Ethnology Bulletin* 43, Smithsonian Institute, Washington, D.C.

THOMAS, EDWIN N.
1960 Some Comments on the Functional Bases for Small Iowa Towns. *Iowa Business Digest* 31(2):10-16.

1967 Additional Comments on Population Size Relationships for Sets of Cities. In *Quantitative Geography Part I: Economic and Cultural Topics,* edited by W. L. Garrison and D. F. Marble, pp. 167-190. Northwestern University Studies in Geography Number 14. Northwestern University, Evanston, Illinois.

THWAITES, REUBEN GOLD
1900 *The Jesuit Relations and Allied Documents,* Vol. 68. Burrows Brothers Co, Cleveland.

TRIGGER, BRUCE
1990 Monumental Architecture: A Thermodynamic Explanation of Symbolic Behavior. *World Archaeology* 22(2):119-132.

VINING, RUTLEDGE
1955 A Description of Certain Spatial Aspects of an Economic System. *Economic Development and Cultural Change* 3:147-195.

VOORHIES, BARBARA
1976 *The Chantuto People: An Archaic Period Society of the Chiapas Littoral, Mexico.* Papers of the New World Archaeological Society, No. 41, Brigham Young University, Provo.

1989a   A Model of the Pre-Aztec Political System of Soconusco. In *Ancient Trade and Tribute: Economies of the Soconusco Region of Mesoamerica,* edited by Barbara Voorhies, pp. 95-129. University of Utah Press, Salt Lake City.

1989b   Settlement Patterns in the Western Soconusco: Methods of Site Recovery and Dating Results. In *New Frontiers in the Archaeology of the Pacific Coast of Southern Mesoamerica,* edited by Frederick Bové and Lynette Heller. Anthropological Research Papers No.3, pp. 103-124. Arizona State University, Tempe.

2004   *Coastal Collectors in the Holocene: The Chantuto People of Southwest Mexico.* University Press of Florida, Gainesville.

VOORHIES, BARBARA AND JANINE GASCO
1984   El período Postclásico Tardío de Acapetahua, Chiapas, México. In *Investigaciones recientes en el área Maya, Tomo 1,* pp. 431-438. Sociedad Mexicana de Antropología, San Cristobal de las Casas, Chiapas.

2004   *Postclassic Soconusco Society: The Late Prehistory of the Coast of Chiapas, Mexico.* Institute for Mesoamerican Studies, State University of New York, Albany.

VOORHIES, BARBARA AND DOUGLAS J. KENNETT
1995   Buried Sites on the Soconusco Coastal Plain, Chiapas, Mexico. *Journal of Field Archaeology* 22: 65-79.

VOORHIES, BARBARA, DOUGLAS J. KENNETT, JOHN G. JONES, AND THOMAS A. WAKE
2002   A Middle Archaic Archaeological Site on the West Coast of Mexico. *Latin American Antiquity* 13:179-200.

WASELKOV, GREGORY
1987   Shellfish Gathering and Shell Midden Archaeology. In *Advances in Archaeological and Method and Theory, Vol. 11.* edited by Michael Schiffer, pp. 93-210. Academic Press, San Diego.

WEBSTER, DAVID (EDITOR)
1989   *The House of the Bacabs, Copan, Honduras.* Dumbarton Oaks, Washington, D.C.

WEIGAND, PHIL C.
1985   Evidence for Complex Societies During the Western Mesoamerican Classic Period. In *The Archaeology of West and Northwest Mesoamerica,* edited by Michael S. Foster and Phil C. Weigand, pp. 47-92. Westview Press, Boulder.

ZIPF, GEORGE KINGSLEY
1932   *Selected Studies of the Principle of Relative Frequency in Language.* Harvard University Press, Cambridge.

1949   *Human Behavior and the Principle of Least Effort: An Introduction to Human Ecology.* Addison-Wesley, Cambridge.